PRAISE FOR BRAD LOMENICK AND
THE CATALYST LEADER

The Catalyst Leader is a must read for the next generation of influencers. Brad provides practical application for leaders at all levels to lead well and lead now.

— John C. Maxwell, cofounder, Catalyst; *New York Times* best-selling author

"Called, but not yet equipped." Now there's a phrase I can relate to. That's how my friend Brad Lomenick describes his initiation into the world of leadership. Little did he know that his discipline and faithfulness would eventually land him in a role that would give him the opportunity to influence tens of thousands of emerging leaders in the U.S. and around the world. *The Catalyst Leader* is a must-read for next-gen leaders who want to start strong, end strong, and change their worlds along the way.

— Andy Stanley, senior pastor, North Point Ministries

In *The Catalyst Leader*, Brad Lomenick shares eight essentials for becoming a change maker—a young leader who has the potential to dramatically impact the world for the sake of the Kingdom. I highly recommend this book to those who are passionate about the calling God has placed on their lives.

— Jim Daly, president, Focus on the Family

Not surprisingly, Brad walks deftly between vision and reality, stirring an ache and a resolve in the hearts of leaders. This is one of the *best* books I've read on leadership in recent memory. It is a clear, compelling, and stirring call to leaders everywhere.

— Nancy Ortberg, author, *Non-Linear Leadership*

The Catalyst Leader is an amazing guide for the purposeful culture maker, and intentional game changer. This book is for people who live to make good things happen.

— Charles Jenkins, senior pastor, Fellowship
Missionary Baptist Church

Brad Lomenick offers a treasure trove of leadership knowledge that you can't afford to not cash in on. This book contains the kind of transformative insights and truths that guarantee you'll become a stronger, more innovative leader.

— Margaret Feinberg, author, *Wonderstruck*
and *Scouting the Divine;* www.
margaretfeinberg.com

Brad Lomenick is a leader of leaders. He's also one of the nicest people I know, which is a highly underrated quality of great leaders! I'm a huge fan of the Catalyst Conference and *The Catalyst Leader.* Without Brad's investment in my life as a leader, I know I wouldn't be where I am today.

— Mark Batterson, lead pastor, National
Community Church; best-selling author,
The Circle Maker and *Soul Print*

It is a widely known fact that today's emerging young leaders are not content with status quo . . . to simply rest on past successes and/or mediocre results. Rather, these young "movers and shakers" in today's society are deeply passionate, highly motivated men and women who think globally, are armed with the latest technology, and are determined to make an immediate and lasting difference in their world. And they are avid readers and learners. *The Catalyst Leader* by Brad Lomenick is an honest, candid look at eight leadership "essentials," packed with snippets of stories and practical advice from top leaders, and is, frankly, one of the best books on leadership in the market today. If you are called to be an effective influencer in any capacity, then this book is for you!

— Dr. Wess Stafford, president and CEO,
Compassion International; author, *Too
Small to Ignore* and *Just a Minute*

I've seen and experienced the Catalyst leadership and Brad in action and up close. It's the real deal, and so is this book. We need a new generation of change makers, and *The Catalyst Leader* outlines the keys for making a difference now.

— Mark Burnett, award-winning executive
producer and creator, *The Voice*, *Survivor*,
Apprentice, and *Shark Tank*

No one is more qualified to write a book on leadership than the leader of Catalyst, a leadership movement helping to shape and inspire the next generation of leaders. I've been waiting for this book from Brad, and he's given us great insight with loads of practical application. This is a strong addition to your leadership library.

— Christine Caine, cofounder, A21
Campaign; author, *Undaunted*

Brad Lomenick is one of the best leaders I know. His book, *The Catalyst Leader* unpacks years of invaluable leadership wisdom. Whether you are a beginning leader or a seasoned one, this book will unquestionably make you better.

— Craig Groeschel, senior pastor,
LifeChurch.tv; author, *Altar Ego*

This is the fastest-moving, most exciting time in the history of business. Incredible opportunities are flying past us at breakneck speed, and once they're gone, they're gone. But if you don't have the spiritual and emotional foundation for growing as a leader, those opportunities will roll right over you. Brad Lomenick has become a master at preparing young leaders for the opportunities and challenges they'll face, and I'm fired up that he's poured everything he's learned about growing leaders into *The Catalyst Leader*.

— Dave Ramsey, *New York Times* best selling
author; nationally syndicated radio show
host

For years, Brad Lomenick has been one of the people who have helped me navigate the tricky waters of leadership and influence. I'm thrilled that now he's taking that same wisdom and making it available to so many people in the form of this book.

— Jon Acuff, *Wall Street Journal* best-selling author, *Quitter* and *Stuff Christians Like*

I am called to be a leader of a national organization, but I don't always feel fully equipped. I suspect you've felt this way too. Most of us wish there was a roadmap of essential practices to help us lead well, navigate the pitfalls of success, avoid burnout, and really become a change maker. *The Catalyst Leader* is that roadmap and fresh leadership voice for which we've been looking. Brilliantly written by my friend, Brad Lomenick, this research-based book is innovative, practical, and refreshingly authentic. I highly recommend this resource!

— Lysa TerKeurst, *New York Times* best-selling author, *Made to Crave* and *Unglued*; president, Proverbs 31 Ministries

This book by Brad Lomenick is way overdue! What he has seen and experienced as a leader of the Catalyst movement has now been brought to life for us in the pages that follow. Get a highlighter and a cup of coffee and carve out some time to learn. I can promise you will be stretched and challenged.

— Perry Noble, senior pastor, NewSpring Church; *New York Times* best-selling author, *Unleash!*

There are people who are affected by change and those who effect change. My new friend, Brad Lomenick, is one who God has entrusted to affect change in biblical leadership across our country. He knows what he's talking about when it comes to leadership because he's seen it and he's living it. Get this book for yourself and the young leaders in your church or organization. Read it, and apply it to your leadership and thinking.

— Dr. James MacDonald, senior pastor, Harvest Bible Chapel; author, *Vertical Church*

With *The Catalyst Leader*, Brad has assembled a resource that will prove invaluable for emerging and established leaders alike. There are few people who have done more to inspire and equip leaders to make an impact in what matters most—in work and in life.

— Scott Belsky, cofounder, Behance; author,
Making Ideas Happen

Brad Lomenick is an incredible leader who has spent his life learning from incredible leaders. He's zeroed in on the most important aspects of leadership and given a brilliant roadmap for growth and development. This is a fantastic leadership book I can't wait to share with our team!

— Jud Wilhite, author, *Pursued*; senior
pastor, Central Christian Church

Brad has a passion and ability to develop young leaders like few people I have ever met. I am continually inspired by his love for God, his heart for the church, and his wisdom for strategic leadership. This book is more than a list of leadership principles. It's a call to become the influencer and change maker you were meant to be. It's a challenge to be strong in the grace of God that is on your life. This book comes straight from Brad's heart, and it will forever alter the way you lead.

— Judah Smith, pastor, City Church; author,
Jesus Is ___.

The Catalyst movement continues to impact leaders all around the world, and Brad's leadership has been instrumental in that impact. In *The Catalyst Leader*, Brad provides insight and practical advice for leaders looking to truly become Catalysts in their communities, and ultimately change makers.

— Israel Houghton, Grammy-winning artist,
songwriter, and worship leader

In this book, Brad shares lessons he's learned through his own leadership successes and failures and wisdom from a wide variety of older leaders. He offers practical advice to help young leaders shape sustainable ministries and live lives of integrity. I hope this book will be widely read!

— Lynne Hybels, Advocate for Global
Engagement, Willow Creek Community
Church

No one knows next generation leaders better than Brad Lomenick. As the Lead Visionary and President of Catalyst, he has convened, inspired, and equipped hundreds of thousands of Christian leaders. In *The Catalyst Leader*, Brad provides a practical framework for taking your leadership to the next level and insuring that it is both effective and relevant.

> — Michael Hyatt, *New York Times* best-selling author, *Platform: Get Noticed in a Noisy World*; former chairman and CEO, Thomas Nelson Publishers

I've had the great honor of working with Brad Lomenick at several Catalyst conferences, and have been in awe of his strong leadership and his pursuit of creativity and excellence in all he does. I know and respect many of the leaders profiled here, and am confident that you'll be inspired by their stories and ideas.

> — Scott Harrison, founder, Charity: Water

I defy anyone to read this book and not be inspired. Brad knows leaders, he knows the need for leadership, and he knows the particular kinds of leaders that will be required for the coming generation. A great, informed, motivating, practical, life-directing read. Read it before you get any older.

> — John Ortberg, senior pastor, Menlo Park Presbyterian Church; author, *Who Is This Man?*

Having spoken at Catalyst, I can attest that it is a movement that is incredibly effective at leading leaders. Brad has done us a great favor by writing this book to share what Jesus has taught him while leading this movement. I deeply appreciate Brad as a leader, and am thankful for this book.

> — Pastor Mark Driscoll, founder, Mars Hill Church and Resurgence; cofounder, Acts 29 Church Planting

Do you feel called to lead? *The Catalyst Leader* reveals the core truths about what it takes to be an effective leader, and how to uncover the gifts and talents you possess and put them to work serving others.

> — Daniel H. Pink, author, *To Sell is Human* and *Drive*

Leading is hard, but Lomenick's book will put you on the path to success. *The Catalyst Leader* is the definitive guide to sparking change within your organization—and your life. Be a catalyst for change. Learn to lead.

— Claire Diaz Ortiz, social innovation
director, Twitter; author, *Twitter for Good*

Brad Lomenick presents a detailed blueprint to effect change and lead with integrity. *The Catalyst Leader* will help the reader to approach the immense task of leadership with the principles and lessons through which daily battles are won. For anyone looking to make an impact on their community, I would highly recommend this book.

— Matthew Barnett, cofounder, Dream Center

Brad Lomenick understands next generation leadership. Whether young or old, get ready for your leadership to be taken to a new level.

— Rick Warren, pastor, Saddleback Church;
best-selling author, *The Purpose Driven Life*

Brad has captured some of the most elusive and fundamental lessons of leadership in a readable and actionable way. Any hungry leader will find plenty to chew on here!

— Patrick Lencioni, president, The Table
Group; best-selling author, *The Five
Dysfunctions of a Team* and *The Advantage*

Brad Lomenick is at the fountainhead of an emerging wave of next generation influencers. From his unique position as shepherd of the world's premier young leaders conference, Brad speaks the language of (and wisdom to) those who are busy believing they can actually do the kind of good that reshapes a broken world. You'll be glad you let him speak to you, and, young or old, you'll be inspired to be more of the leader you were meant to be.

— Louie Giglio, founder, Passion City Church
and The Passion Movement

A practical handbook, roadmap and guide for the next generation of influencers. An essential resource for leaders at all levels.

— Joel Houston, co-lead pastor, Hillsong
Church NYC; creative director, Hillsong
Church

THE

8 ESSENTIALS FOR

CATALYST

BECOMING A CHANGE MAKER

LEADER

BRAD LOMENICK

THOMAS NELSON

Since 1798

NASHVILLE   DALLAS   MEXICO CITY   RIO DE JANEIRO

Published in Nashville, Tennessee, by Thomas Nelson. Thomas Nelson is a registered trademark of Thomas Nelson, Inc.

Thomas Nelson, Inc., titles may be purchased in bulk for educational, business, fund-raising, or sales promotional use. For information, please e-mail SpecialMarkets@ThomasNelson.com.

Published in association with Christopher Ferebee, attorney and literary agent, www.christopherferebee.com.

Unless otherwise noted, Scripture quotations are taken from the NEW AMERICAN STANDARD BIBLE®, © The Lockman Foundation 1960, 1962, 1963, 1968, 1971, 1972, 1973, 1975, 1977, 1995. Used by permission.

Scripture quotations marked NIV are taken from the Holy Bible, New International Version®, © 1973, 1978, 1984, 2011 by Biblica, Inc.™ Used by permission of Zondervan. All rights reserved worldwide. www.zondervan.com.

Names and identifying details of some people mentioned in this book have been changed to protect their privacy.

The websites and organizations recommended in this book are intended as resources for the reader. These websites and organizations are not intended in any way to be or to imply an endorsement on behalf of Thomas Nelson, nor does the publisher vouch for their content for the life of this book.

ISBN 978-1-4002-7669-1 (IE)

Library of Congress Control Number: 2012953157

ISBN: 978-1-59555-497-0

Printed in the United States of America

13 14 15 16 17 RRD 6 5 4 3 2 1

To my parents, Jerry and Penny, who modeled these leadership essentials for me. Words can't adequately express my appreciation for your love, dedication, and sacrifice on my behalf. You are my heroes.

CONTENTS

A NOTE
FROM BRAD

I'M PASSIONATE ABOUT RAISING UP GREAT LEADERS AROUND the globe, and I've devoted much of my life to convening, equipping, and developing people of all ages and stages in life who want to grow in their leadership abilities. If you've picked up this book, I suspect you fit that label. You are in a position of some level of influence, and you're looking for guidance on how you can better steward the opportunities you've been given.

Leading in this century is a daunting task. The digital age increased the availability of information, but not all of it is worth consuming. We are connected in unprecedented ways, but technology doesn't always allow us space to incubate and mature as individuals and as leaders.

I've written *The Catalyst Leader* to empower you to lead better and longer. I'm hopeful that you can be great; but greatness takes work. You've been handed a set of keys, but you must learn how to drive responsibly. To avoid road hazards and take the correct streets. To learn when to press ahead and when to pull over. So I've attempted to give you a trustworthy road map—sketched with insider stories from my experience of leading Catalyst, one of America's largest networks and gatherers of young leaders—and to offer practical advice you can incorporate into your life and work.

My goal is not to coerce you to operate like Catalyst or to convince you to mimic our every operating procedure. Rather, I want to provide you with essential practices that have served us well over the years as we've taken the same journey you now travel.

Like many young leaders, you want to make a difference. To make your life's work count. To leave the world better than you found it. Becoming a catalyst leader means becoming a change maker—someone who leverages his or her influence for the betterment of the world, the collective good of others, and the greater glory of God. In order to realize this dream, I believe you must:

- discover God's unique calling on your life;
- embrace your true identity and share it with others;
- develop an insatiable hunger for a vibrant relationship with God;
- chase after a level of excellence that will stretch you and astonish others;
- learn to push through fear and take risks;
- root yourself in unchanging principles rather than shifting circumstances;
- create and cast a compelling vision for the future; and
- build bridges with others for the purpose of learning and cooperating.

This is possible by developing the eight essentials for becoming a change maker that I'll share with you. Keep in mind that you cannot pick and choose from this list. An individual who develops only five or six of these characteristics is not a catalyst leader. That's why they are called *essentials*, not strengths. You must commit to them all.

This might sound intimidating to some, but I have a feeling it excites you. Why?

Because you're a leader.

You know well the challenges that come with your calling. You nurture no illusions of easy roads or shortcuts. You are willing to work hard to forge a legacy so when you survey your life in fifty or sixty years, you will know that you've not only led *now,* but you've also led *well.* Only through leading well can one finish well.

So welcome to your journey toward becoming a catalyst leader.

It begins right now.

—Brad Lomenick

President and Lead Visionary,
Catalyst, Atlanta, Georgia

INTRODUCTION

LEARNING TO LEAD

A FRIEND ONCE TOLD ME THAT FOLLOWING IS EASY BUT LEADING is difficult. I knew he was right, but it wasn't until I was thirty-three years old that the truth of his words truly took root in my own life.

I was consulting with INJOY, an organization founded by John Maxwell—one of the greatest leadership experts of the last quarter-century. INJOY's leadership team birthed an idea for a young leaders' conference, and fifteen hundred people gathered at the first Catalyst event. When INJOY realized that Catalyst had traction, I was brought in to help write the business plan and conduct the market research for the venture, among other strategic brands within the organization. After only a couple of years, attendance at Catalyst events doubled.

As the event grew, so did my involvement. I joined the team full time shortly after that. But everything changed a few years later when my two friends who had been directing the effort stepped aside to focus on other work. I remember having breakfast with them the day they delivered news of their departure. We met at J. Christopher's, an Atlanta restaurant famous among locals and coincidentally the same place where the three of us had made something of a pact that we were in this thing together. Over the world's tastiest ham-and-cheese omelets, they told me they were leaving. But I felt called to stay.

My drive back to the Catalyst offices was a long one, a blur of traffic lights bathed with a sense of loneliness. I knew there was something still left for me to accomplish at Catalyst, but I didn't know how to do that without my friends. *What if I fail? What if the event flops? Can I do this on my own? If not, will I regret my decision to stay?*

I pulled my silver Dodge Durango truck into the warehouse that doubled as our headquarters. Then I took a deep breath, slipped into my office, and shut the door. Plopping down in my chair, I felt more alone than I could remember. Fate had handed me a responsibility that exceeded my years, and one I wasn't sure I was prepared for. We expected nine thousand attendees at our event that year, and sixty thousand more simulcasting another event we helped produce. Our founder, John Maxwell, popped into my mind. And who was I? Some kid from Oklahoma who ended up at the helm of this massive ship by accident?

As I counted all the ceiling tiles above me, and the obligations that now fell solely on me, I felt confident that I had been called to this work. I had twelve years of leadership experience under my belt and a determination to get the job done. I recognized areas where the organization needed to improve and sensed a vision for where it should go. But I wasn't sure I was the one for the job, let alone equipped for the task.

Fortunately, that memorable morning in 2005 wasn't the first time I'd felt called but not equipped.

LOST VALLEY RANCH

Twelve years earlier, I experienced a series of disappointments that had left me feeling deflated and searching for my life's calling. I was a junior history major at the University of Oklahoma with a strong desire to step into a leadership role. I'd been a leader all my life, from elementary through high school, culminating in my becoming president of my senior class and captain of the high school football team. Motivated by a deep desire to influence, I decided in college to run for president of my fraternity house. I lost by one vote. Then I ran for president of Interfraternity Council, a body governing all fraternities on campus, and lost by a much larger margin. With the semester ending, I didn't have any plans for the summer, let alone for graduation after my senior year.

I shared my frustrations and questions with my friend

and fraternity brother Jason Shipman, who suggested that I join him working on a dude ranch in Sedalia, Colorado, for the summer. I'd never been to a dude ranch but enjoyed the outdoors and embraced the possibility of a new adventure. With nothing holding me back, I decided to tag along.

A few months later, I arrived at Lost Valley Ranch and soon discovered the history of the place. In 1961, "Big Bob" and Marion Foster purchased the property with the intention to transform it into a world-class Western ranch vacation retreat for families. What they created was every boy's childhood dream—a place where modern-day cowboys drove cattle by day and sang choruses around campfires under starlight. Wild West magic filled the air, while twelve-thousand-foot mountain peaks stood proudly around us. Summer trotted along like my brown-and-white horse, Bandit. As far I was concerned, he was the most amazing steed who'd ever galloped through Pike National Forest.

Those four fairy-tale months brought rest to my weary soul. I sensed God had used my previous misfortunes to lead me to Lost Valley Ranch for a reason, but I had no idea that my summer job was sowing seeds for a new season of life.

After graduating from college the next spring, I knew I wanted to go back to the ranch—even if only for a few months—before returning to Norman for law school at the University of Oklahoma. But once back at Lost Valley the following spring, the months turned into years, and my aspirations of law school melted like the Colorado snow. Not long after I arrived, the ranch foreman, Ben Martin, told me he was leaving soon and wanted me to replace him and manage Lost Valley.

My heart leaped at the opportunity to take the reins of this organization, but I had no idea how to run a dude ranch. This wasn't like a city job, managing a handful of entry-level college graduates from a corner office. Lost Valley boasted one hundred and fifty horses, two hundred head of cattle, one hundred guests, and fifty employees. We were an hour from the nearest town and two hours from the closest veterinarian. But my anxiety paled in comparison to my sense of calling. I quickly agreed to take the position and became the most enthusiastic but least equipped foreman of a four-diamond ranch in America.

Though I didn't know much about what I was doing, I was determined to succeed. I digested handbooks on veterinary medicine and business management. I learned how to lead a team and inspire others by creating an environment of constant personal development. The ranch thrived for four years under my watch, and today I count that period as one of my life's biggest accomplishments.

My promotion at Lost Valley flashed through my mind as I sat silently in my office ten years later. Once again, I was facing a great opportunity that I felt called to accept, but not altogether equipped to handle. Like the college-graduate-turned-cowboy a decade earlier, I had no choice but to find a way forward.

LEADING NOW

Having led an event-driven movement of next-generation leaders for ten years, I know I'm not the only one who's had this experience. I've discovered many men and women who are called-but-not-yet-equipped and are influencing churches, businesses, and nonprofits across America. Innovative and passionate, they still need guidance if they are to reach their potential.

As I've dialogued with young leaders, the common characteristic I'm finding is the desire to lead *now*. They're embarking on creative projects, starting new organizations, writing books, and excelling in large corporations. These individuals don't want to climb the ladder; they want to catapult into positions of influence. Energetic and passionate, young leaders want to jump in and make a difference *now*.

Perhaps vocational eagerness grips rising influencers more than previous generations because of the unique opportunities of the twenty-first century. Fifty years ago, young people were forced to "wait their turn" while their elders aged out of corner offices and boardrooms and pulpits. Today, however, organizations are opening positions to the fresh thinking and idealism that young people possess.

My thirty-one-year-old friend Garrett started a production company that makes short films. In only a few years, his movies have been used across the country to raise awareness of global poverty and injustice. My colleague Chris became executive director of an international organization with half a dozen intentional communities while in his twenties. Another friend of mine, David, was called to pastor a congregation in crisis at twenty-seven and now leads a thriving megachurch that is shaping the future of world missions. My heart fills with hope and expectation at what God wants to accomplish through the younger generation.

Perhaps never before have so many young leaders been poised for influence. Scores of twenty- and thirty-somethings are running companies, nonprofits, churches, and social innovation projects. They don't have ten to fifteen years to figure things out anymore; they need to be equipped and prepared *now*.

LEADING WELL

Today's young leaders grew up with a grasp of technology that is essential for organizational success. As an educated and diverse generation, they think globally. Modern organizations need these qualities as a complement to seasoned workers in order to compete in our changing world.[1] For better or worse, young people can grasp life's reins earlier than ever before.

In addition, social media and the Internet provide opportunities to start new initiatives, build a following, and make a difference. Decades ago, the normative path was to wait in line and plod along en route to the gold watch. Now one can launch an organization with an inexpensive website to capture a large audience and let them vote on the quality of their idea. The path to influence has been truncated as many leaders today are circumventing the usual channels to realize their callings earlier. Many have platforms that exceed their wisdom, experience, or maturity. Our generation needs a roadmap for leading *well*.

Jon Acuff grew up loving to write and began his career as a copy editor for YellowBook.com. In his spare time, he ran a Christian satire blog called "Stuff Christians Like."[2] People began to resonate with his content, and soon his blog became one of the most popular Christian sites on the web. He began speaking all over the country while continuing to write and edit business copy.

When radio host Dave Ramsey encountered Jon's work, he offered him a job as one of his key team members. Jon accepted and finally left his position as a copy editor. As Jon shares in his recent book, *Quitter: Closing the Gap between Your Day Job and Your Dream Job*, he feels more fulfilled today than ever.[3] He is also glad he gets to put his talents to use every single day.

Jon reminded me recently that we must never compare our beginning to someone else's ending. Instead, we need to seek God's plan for us as He reveals our callings to us. It's important we focus on what God has called each of us to do, and not compare our callings to others'.

But contemporary culture is pushing into positions of

influence people who are unequipped for the task they've been given. Some of my best friends sit atop great organizations but fail to shepherd their teams and lead these entities well. I think of Billy, who founded an innovative media company a few years back. They produce amazing work but have been bogged down in low morale resulting from a lack of compassionate and capable leadership. Though Billy's excitement for the work is contagious, his organization battles high turnover rates.

I've begun to see a disappointing pattern among young leaders. They achieve liftoff with a rocket start but quickly fizzle out. Their early success, when the world hung at their fingertips, ends almost as quickly as it began. Ethical failures. Team disintegration. Financial disaster. Family problems. With each instance of short-lived success, I grow further convinced that we need to nurture leaders who will not just lead *now* but also lead *well*. When people lead well, they are more likely to finish well.

Often I fall into the same snares. Driven by my vision for Catalyst and my own personal ambitions, I tend to lose focus of those around me. Many times I don't display the eight essentials of leading well, as my employees can attest. But the goal is not *perfection* but rather a *posture* of moving toward healthy habits and characteristics. Forgetting these essentials can destroy an influencer.

My friend Sandra started a nonprofit on the West Coast to help the unemployed attain an education and locate work.

But her unbridled sense of ambition was not matched in accountability and support, so her promising career ended in moral failure. I often wonder how her story would have been different if she had focused on leading well.

I could list dozens of others like my friend Matt who planted a church with a promising congregation and a talented leadership team. His church grew steadily, but these young hopefuls and their thirty-five-year-old pastor weren't prepared for the challenges of church planting. Like so many others, they burned out or left within a few years.

The usual suspects of downfall include unmet expectations, personal failure, and overwhelming stress, but underlying them all is a need to prepare rising influencers as they realize their callings. Some can manage being called-but-not-equipped until they find their way; but for others, it is deadly. Ambition must be grounded in wisdom. Inspiration must be pursued with integrity. Dreams must be built with boundaries. And passions need the steady hand of principles to guide them.

LEAVING A MARK

The good news is that many young influencers are leading well. I've spent over a decade on the new frontier of Christian leadership and have been overwhelmed by many who are placing longevity ahead of opportunity. These influencers express the eight essentials that empower them to avoid the greatest pitfalls as they find solutions to our world's problems and live lives that matter.

Today's influencers recognize their callings and are passionate for God. They are competent and courageous, authentic and principled, hopeful about the future and unafraid to collaborate with others. Because they've chosen integrity over immediacy, they're accomplishing both and setting an example for the rest of us. You'll meet many of them in the pages that follow, and my hope is that their stories will inspire you to tread a better path.

To get a fuller picture of what today's Christian leaders look like, I've partnered with Barna Research Group. Through a series of questions, we were able to probe the thoughts, opinions, and passions of 1,116 self-identified Christians ages eighteen and older. (The results of this "Today's Christian Leaders" study are included in the appendix.) Our findings were surprising but informative about the future of leadership among those who follow Jesus. My hope is to combine this empirical data with anecdotal insights to empower you to become a change maker wherever you find yourself.

Interestingly, our research showed that 82 percent of Christians today agree "the nation is facing a crisis of leadership because there are not enough good leaders right now." Like me, most understand the difficult challenges influencers in this century face and the need for more people who are able to lead better, longer. This book is to help the 82 percent become the answer to our current leadership crisis.

I wish I could say that I walked out of my office that significant morning in 2005 and led with excellence. But I'd be lying. Times when I should have taken a risk, I played it safe. Other times, I gambled and lost. Often I get so wrapped up in blind ambition and accomplishing things on my to-do list that I forget to acknowledge those around me who deserve a lion's share of the credit. I've made decisions that I now see were mistakes, and I've failed more times than I can count.

I think of the time I made an off-the-cuff and inappropriate remark about an attendee from the stage at a Catalyst event. I knew I'd committed an error, but there was no fixing it. And then there was an event a few years back where I unilaterally decided to redesign the ending to our last session despite the warnings of my team. I pushed it through without considering their opinions simply because I could. It flopped, and I learned a valuable lesson.

But I committed one of my most grievous mistakes one particularly frustrating July morning. I had arrived at the office on time to find that everyone on the team was late. Without pausing to think, I fired off a scathing e-mail to everyone. Unfortunately, my condescending note arrived in their inboxes at a time when they were tired, stressed, and working on empty. My thoughtless attempt to motivate turned into mutiny. Two interns were so upset by my comments they burst into tears, and several team members almost quit upon arrival. Thankfully one of my most trusted coworkers confronted me, and I apologized at our next team meeting. I learned that the right thing said in the wrong way is the wrong thing.

These stories of failure illustrate that I am an imperfect leader. I've discovered many of these essentials the hard way. I'm penning this book in part so you can avoid the mistakes I've made as you continue to learn to lead.

Catalyst has been blessed with a poised and gifted team that carries our organization through when I don't. As a result, we have grown from producing one event per year to nine annual events, and now over thirty thousand influencers gather each year under the Catalyst banner to encounter creative ideas, fresh thinking, spiritual wisdom, and much-needed encouragement.

Catalyst is a passionate community of hundreds of thousands of young leaders who look to us for inspiration, equipping, and practical leadership help. Since 2000, over two hundred thousand leaders have convened in arenas, churches, and convention centers, and millions more through our online community and resources. The movement of Catalyst far exceeds my initial vision and imagination. Through my experiences, I've encountered many leaders and noticed the characteristics common among the most effective influencers. In this book, I pass along these observations and reflections to you.

Like me, your gut is rumbling with the compulsion to influence, to make a difference, to leave a mark. I'm convinced there are thousands of leaders just like the thirty-three-year-old version of me, and perhaps you are one of them. You find yourself sitting in an empty office, door closed, counting obligations. You know you've been called to the work you're doing, but you crave the wisdom to lead well. I'm passing along to you what I've learned from my journey and the expeditions of others so that you will avoid common mistakes and snares as you pursue your vocation.

My friend was right: leading *is* difficult. Yet the need is much greater. As God unfolds the possibilities and opportunities sitting at our fingertips, may we not just lead now, but lead well.

CALLED

FIND YOUR UNIQUENESS

> When you live your life knowing the mission and calling and
> voice of God in your soul and you know where that compass
> is driving you forward, you will become a rare commodity in a
> world searching for direction.
>
> **—ERWIN MCMANUS, CATALYST WEST**

LOOKING BACK IN OUR LIVES, WE CAN OFTEN IDENTIFY THE
moments when our gifts were beginning to bubble up and
point us toward God's callings for us. I remember the day
my mother dropped me off at my first-grade class. Bristow,
Oklahoma, is a small town of five thousand, not far from
Tulsa. Since my dad was principal of the middle school and
knew all the teachers in the school system, he informed me

weeks earlier that Mrs. Weaver would be my first-grade teacher. With a new pair of jeans, a *Brady Bunch* lunchbox, and a bowl haircut, I was ready to conquer the world. Or Bristow Elementary School at least.

Mom was proud—reminding me at least a dozen times to behave and play nicely with the other kids—but she was also emotional. I was filled with excitement. Even at this young age, the thought of connecting with others energized me. Walking into the classroom, I hung my backpack on the coat hook, located my desk, and began memorizing my classmates' names. In hindsight, this was probably the first sign of my calling as a leader.

These passions continued to surface with each passing year. I became one of the captains of the football team in third grade and landed the lead role of Pecos Bill in the school play in sixth grade, the same year I was elected class president.

One memory of elementary school was a showdown regarding the lunch menu in the cafeteria. Our lunchroom only served chocolate milkshakes, and I was convinced that lunch would not be complete without both vanilla and strawberry. I led the student council to victory in the milkshake showdown, and though some might say our win was due to my dad being the principal of the middle school, I claim it was my fearless and staunch stance in the face of opposition!

Even in those elementary moments, I sensed a compelling urge to lead, like a rumble in my gut. Maybe you know the feeling. Something inside is pushing you to the edge, to the front of the line, to make a difference, to leave a mark. From first grade in Mrs. Weaver's class trying to make sure everyone knew each other, to eighth grade when I led the charge for a new school dance. I again felt the rumble in middle school when I was elected student council president. I experienced it in high school when I became senior class president.

During my formative years, I attempted to lead in whatever I did, from school plays, to the classroom, to becoming one of the captains of the football and basketball teams. I desired to be out in front.

My sophomore year of high school, two friends and I started a rap group. I dropped beats under the name Crème-L—a name I was actually proud of at the time—and our trio committed to make a difference through our "music." When the "Don't lay your trash on Oklahoma" anti-litter campaign launched, we wrote a song for it called, "Clean Up the Streets." We performed it in front of the governor and House of Representatives. I'm sure the tape of our performance is tucked away somewhere, and I'm more certain that I'll never let anyone find it.

Approaching my senior year of high school, I began to ponder career paths. My friends and I dreamed about the great accomplishments waiting for us. Some wanted to become teachers and football coaches. Others desired to become doctors or business managers or cattle ranchers.

When it came time to share the dream for my life, a clear answer evaded me. I knew I loved connecting with others and convening people and investing in leaders, but that wasn't a job description. Could I do that in politics or education or business? Perhaps. All I knew was that I felt called to lead.

Graduation day finally arrived, and since I served as senior class president, I had to announce 130 graduates' names—first, middle, and last—as they walked across the stage. The music played and procession began. I stepped up to the microphone without any notes and called out each name from memory. To many who were there, reciting all the names by memory seemed like quite an accomplishment. But for me, it was normal, since I felt a connection to all of my classmates. When the final name was called, my mind flashed back to first grade and I recognized a pattern that had been emerging all along. Looking back, the most important treasure I received that day wasn't a diploma, but rather a glimpse of my calling.

Though I didn't realize it at the time, God had been plotting my path. He opened up doors in college to develop networks of future leaders. I convened members of rival fraternities and sororities for a regular Bible study. I was gifted as a connector, someone who brings people together and equips them to work toward a common purpose. I'd go on to exercise these gifts and my calling through my work in magazines, media, web content, hospitality, and conferences.

KNOW YOUR CALLING

Every Christian has two callings in life: a spiritual one to salvation and also a vocational calling. Life is too short to miss either one. Your two callings are separate but inseparable. The first informs the way you'll live out your second calling. The realization of what Christ has done for us produces a compulsion to live for Him. When we talk about one's "calling," we're speaking about the vocational kind that answers this question: "I've decided to follow God, but how does He want me to use my gifts and passions?"

In the years since my high school graduation, I've come to realize that living one's calling is a necessary first step to leading well and becoming a change maker wherever God has planted you. Without understanding your purpose, you'll end up bogged down in the mud of life. But when you are living out your calling, your work will be better, and you will naturally want to work harder. That's why Catalyst has incorporated calling into our events and organizational fabric.

Our team works hard to create spaces where leaders can hear from God about His direction for their lives. We handpick speakers with great visions who will challenge attendees to discover the visions in their own hearts. If participants come to a Catalyst event not knowing what God might have planned for their lives and leave without inching any closer to that purpose, then we've failed as a team.

We've found that participants often have the opposite

experience. We hear from scores of people each year who say they were encouraged to fully pursue their callings because of a Catalyst event. Each year, handfuls of people sit on one of our couches and thank our team for the emphasis we've placed on this important topic. Oftentimes, attendees were already making a huge impact through their work or ministry, but our event created a space where they could dream about even greater goals.

Similarly, when someone joins our team, we want to make sure he or she is on this journey too. My desire in the first year of a team member's employment is either to affirm the employee's calling or to release the person to pursue it elsewhere. I've set this goal because I desire for Catalyst's heartbeat—both internally and externally—to be equipping the next generation of Christian influencers to discover God's plan for them. Without knowledge of one's calling, leading well is impossible.

God's interaction with His followers throughout the Bible seems to indicate that He places a high value on calling. He visited Moses through a burning bush, spoke to Samuel through a midnight echo, disrupted Paul through a roadside encounter, and gave visions to John in a remote cave. While modern Christians may not encounter God in the same ways, I believe God wants to share His plans for us and inspire us to passionately pursue our purposes. And whenever God speaks—however He chooses—it's always a miracle.

As I have surveyed some of today's rising Christian

leaders, I've discovered a profound thing they share in common: *leaders who make the biggest impact also have the strongest sense of calling.* They seem to know the direction God has marked out for them, and they're chasing after it.

Britt Merrick is one of those leaders. As a teenager, Britt planned to take over Channel Islands Surfboards, his dad's iconic company. His father, Al, is a legend in the industry. Britt grew up in the surfing industry, hanging with the famous clients of his family's company, including the most decorated surfer ever, Kelly Slater. But once he reached his midtwenties, Britt decided to follow Jesus, and his plans shifted.

He began to sense that God was calling him to plant and pastor a church. Britt questioned the intuition since he seemed primed for another path. After much prayer, however, he decided to run after what he believed was his personal calling. Twelve years later, he leads one of the most innovative and influential churches on the West Coast. His church, Reality, is impacting the West Coast and California's surf culture in a way no other church could. But Britt is only one of many leaders who are passionate about living their purpose.

Katie Davis is another. In 2007, at nineteen years old, she traveled to Uganda to teach kindergarten at an orphanage. She never returned home. She felt God pushing her toward that country and its children. Today, she runs an orphanage and a child-sponsorship program that provides hundreds of children with education, food, medical care, and Christian discipleship. The founder of Amazima Ministries, Katie is now a single mother, having adopted fourteen Ugandan children as her own. It would have been easier for Katie to finish college and pursue the American dream, but God had something better in store for her.

After hearing Katie share her story at our Catalyst Atlanta event, I decided to create a scholarship fund to send Katie's fourteen Ugandan children to college. I felt strongly prompted by God to do something more for Katie and her family in that moment. I decided while walking back onto the stage after Katie's interview to create the Katie Davis Scholarship Fund. Katie responds,

> People tell me I am brave. People tell me I am strong. People tell me good job. Well here is the truth of it: I am really not that brave, I am not really that strong, and I am not doing anything spectacular. I am just doing what God czalled me to do as a follower of Him. Feed His sheep, do unto the least of His people.[1]

When I decided to create the scholarship fund, I had no idea how we would accomplish it, but I truly wanted to live out the principle of putting others above ourselves. The Catalyst team was so impressed by what Katie had accomplished at such a young age, we felt moved to act. This is an example of the way we want others to be highlighted at our Catalyst events—we want to be focused and intentional about celebrating others. In fact, royalties from this book will be used to help fund Katie's children going to college, along with several other strategic charitable projects we want to fund through the proceeds.

A Lifetime of Leading Well: Wess Stafford

Wess Stafford knows his calling and lives it without apology. As president of Compassion International, he has devoted his life to caring for children who live in poverty around the world. And he does it in Jesus' name.

I first met Wess when he spoke at a Catalyst West event. His sandy brown hair and soft smile hid his status as an internationally recognized advocate for children, whose organization partners with sixty denominations and thousands of local churches. My friend Mike Foster, who had traveled with Wess on a Compassion trip a few months earlier, warned me that meeting Wess would transform my life. I had no idea how right Mike was.

When I introduced myself, Wess offered me a bear hug and a few slaps on the back. With genuine humility, he expressed how honored he was to be a part of our event. As we discussed his work, his deep passion for God and unwavering commitment to Jesus and the children he serves poured out of him. As he spoke, I found myself wanting to be like him. To live like him. To pursue my own calling with as much tenacity. Wess is one of those people whom you just can't help being inspired by. And the more I got to know Wess, the more I could sense his deep calling to rescue children in Jesus' name. He longs to lift them out of poverty and give them hope.

A member of his staff later told me that when Wess visits a Compassion project, they have a difficult time keeping tabs on him. With the turn of a head, he'll vanish. They'll find him stooped down as low as need be to hug children, conversing with them at eye level. He wants to understand and love those he serves. What an amazing picture of living out the gospel and pursuing a deep sense of purpose.

Wess believes this generation of Christian leaders is going to push extreme poverty off the planet. The son of missionaries to the Ivory Coast, Wess was often heartbroken when his African friends died from cruel realities of a life in poverty. His call to fight these atrocities led him to Compassion in 1977, and he's served as its president since 1993. When Wess felt God stir his heart to care for kids in need, he didn't know how he'd live that out. But there are more than one million children in twenty-six countries who are sure glad he did.

Of course, God doesn't always call His followers to full-time missions or ministry. Consider Scott Harrison. During his twenties, he was one of the top nightclub promoters in New York City. He was earning lots of money, living a glamorous lifestyle, and enjoying the luxuries of the Big Apple. But deep down, he wasn't satisfied. He knew God had wired him to do something else. Something that would affect people around the world and not just in New York's club scene.

When he turned thirty, he made a bold decision to give

up his job and launch an organization called charity:water. Starting a nonprofit was risky, but Scott felt certain this was what God wanted him to do. More than six years later, his organization has provided clean water to millions and has revolutionized the way American charities operate. He hopes to eradicate the global water crisis in the next twenty years. None of it would have been possible without his strong sense of personal calling and the courage to pursue it.

> Our sense of calling should be like an unfolding epic adventure.
>
> —CHRISTINE CAINE, COFOUNDER OF A21 CAMPAIGN

My DVR is set to record *Survivor, Celebrity Apprentice, Shark Tank,* and *The Voice.* Do you know the executive producer behind all of these shows? Mark Burnett. He's become a legend in the entertainment industry over the last fifteen years, often credited with creating the global reality television craze. Now, he and his wife—Roma Downey, *Touched by an Angel* actress and celebrity in her own right—feel called to create a new made-for-TV Bible series project titled *The Bible.* They both feel a sense of purpose and calling to leverage the influence they've created through their careers to share the gospel. I've been able to work together with them to advance this cause, and I count them among the best examples of people living out their faith and calling in the entertainment industry.

Watch Mark Burnett talk about the Bible Project.
http://catalystleader.com/markburnett

Like Britt, Katie, Scott, and Mark, the next generation of Christian influencers is passionate about finding and pursuing their divine purposes. They don't want to work thirty or forty years in a job that fails to fulfill their deepest longings. Instead, this generation wants to find career paths that utilize both their talents and their passions. They are locating and living their callings, and we're all better for it.

TRACKING DOWN YOUR PURPOSE

Sadly, too few leaders today understand their life's purpose. They meander through life, wandering with no sense of where God is leading them. In our study, only 3 percent said that "purpose" was their defining leadership quality. That number fell to a measly 1 percent for those ages 18 to 39. Only about one-third of Christians (34 percent) feel called to the work they currently do. This seems to indicate to me that many young Christian leaders have not found their callings, or at least feel their current work doesn't fulfill them. According to our study, younger Christians are more likely than older Christians to confess they have never even considered the idea of being called to their current role.

Many reasons exist for this travesty. Some simply complicate or mystify the issue. In the last five years, more and more young leaders have often asked me about vocational calling. They realize its importance, are obsessed with finding it, and are frustrated by the hunt. I've found that too many people think of calling as a hidden treasure for which one must search high and low. They feel trapped in a cosmic game of hide-and-seek-my-purpose. Irritation intensifies as they attempt to locate a clearly marked map that can lead them to their life's purpose.

But one's calling isn't a pot of gold to be found at the end of a rainbow. It's not buried deep beneath the ground in unmarked soil. God wants us to use our gifts and passions, and He's placed them in plain sight. Many of us take the perspective that his or her calling is mysterious and a hidden treasure for which there is no map. But I find that God's calling is apparent and more easily identified than we might think.

> Instead of wondering what your next vacation is, maybe
> you should set up a life you don't need to escape from.
> —SETH GODIN, AUTHOR

Kent Humphreys, author, CEO, and business adviser, once told me that your life's calling is usually apparent at an early age, often emerging between the ages of five and nineteen. He encourages people to look back on their childhood and formative years up through their late teens and evaluate what they were passionate about, good at, and drawn to. When I look back over my formative years, I see how those critical leadership moments—from fighting over milkshakes to becoming captain of the football team—shaped me into who I am.

Each of us is embedded with clearly marked instructions for how to accept God's purpose for our lives. These instructions are your talents and passions, and they should not be ignored; for when you combine these two critical components, you unlock the work that God has for you. Calling is not necessarily about a title, position, or even a certain career, but more about a vision and purpose for your life that spans all the seasons of your vocation.

Often a young person—perhaps one of our Catalyst college interns—will approach me and ask, "How can I figure out what I've been called to do?" I respond by asking them to think back over their lives and consider questions like, Which events energized you and which drained you? What projects did you stay up late or get up early to work on? When were you able to do something with ease that might have been difficult for others?

Rather than uncover hidden treasures they didn't know existed, I give them the space to recognize what God has already been revealing in their lives. My advice to people stuck in this rut is always to look back to their childhoods, when the greatest pressures of life still had not found them.

THE PERILS OF AMBITION

Another reason people don't discover their callings is they're too ambitious for their own good. They're too concerned with earning mountains of money or living a comfortable life or being respected or well-known. So they end up pursuing what they *could* do rather than what they *should* do.

I started discovering this truth in college. I settled on a math major during my first two years of school because I thought being a teacher was the right "calling" for me. After all, it was the family business. But once I reached Calculus III, I was miserable. I knew I was running down the wrong path and couldn't imagine spending the rest of my life teaching math, so I decided I should prepare for law school instead by being a history major. I figured that would enable me to make lots of money and achieve notoriety and significance. But that didn't click for me either.

I went to Lost Valley after graduation partly because it seemed heroic. I was good at my job and loved riding horses and getting to play the cowboy, but it still wasn't my true sweet spot. After a few years, the legs of my life seemed to be stuck in mud. I'd dreamed of significance and influence since childhood but had failed to grasp it. I felt called to lead others, but I also felt stuck. Externally, I was happy enough. But internally, I felt a deep and unspoken sense of frustration and disappointment in what I was doing. I wanted to be working on the US Senate floor by the age of twenty-five, but instead, I was scooping manure. Literally.

The frustration was intensified whenever I reconnected with old friends. Several of them had become doctors or lawyers. Others were climbing the corporate ladder at Fortune 500 companies. Unlike me, they were quickly becoming rich and successful. It wasn't until many years later that I realized money and worldly success were not worth pursuing. That's when I grew comfortable with who God created me to be.

I often remind rising leaders that living one's calling may not make you rich or land you on the cover of a magazine. In fact, you may need to blow up your financial standards. Too many people think if they aren't launching a cutting-edge nonprofit or pastoring a large church or sitting in an executive's office at a Fortune 500 company, then maybe they haven't found their purpose. But often they're already living their callings unaware.

Are you engaging your passions in your current career? Are you good at what you do? Do you enjoy your job, or are you just enduring it? Is the greatest intent of your week to get to the weekend? Or to suffer until your next vacation day? Is *what* you do an extension of *who* you are? Many leaders go through life simply enduring what they do, instead of loving it. Sure, life isn't always glamorous or exciting. But do you ever wake up wide-eyed with the expectation that you have opportunities to use the gifts and passions inside of you?

Pursuing one's calling is hard work. For a select few, it will simply appear like manna from God. But for most of us, it takes time and perspective and prayer and periods of wrestling to discern what God has for us. Are you even wrestling? Or are you just waiting for it to appear, to be laid in front of you on a platter?

8 Questions on Calling for a Year-End Review
http://catalystleader.com/eightquestions

Depending on your answers, you may find that you're right where you should be. If so, take the advice of Rick Warren, who encourages people to focus on being faithful in the place and time they are. Let God be responsible for the rest. "Be faithful where you are," he says. "God is responsible for how big your influence gets."[2]

Yet, others *are* on the wrong path, and change is both imminent and necessary. Even the prospect can be paralyzing. In our survey, we asked working Christians if they believed "God is calling them to do something else in terms of work, but they have not been willing to make a change yet because of their current life situation." Nine percent agreed strongly, and another 26 percent agreed somewhat. In other words, more than one in three Christians feel a God-nudge inside of them to do something else with their lives, but haven't found the nerve to pull the trigger.

For some, I suspect fear of the unknown holds them back.

Will I be able to pay my bills if I make a change? Will I be able to succeed in a field I'm not experienced in? For others, the fear of change restrains them. *Life is going pretty well right now. Do I really want to mess things up by changing things?* But many, I think, miss their callings due to fear of finality. *What if I change careers and hate it? I'll be stuck.* But pursuing one's calling isn't a life sentence.

Our generation, perhaps more than previous ones, experiences seasons of calling. My grandfather was a teacher for forty-five years. My dad was in education for forty-five years. But I will probably experience five or six seasons of calling during my vocational life. This is true for my friends and peers, many of whom are "free agents" and are comfortable taking on many short-term projects instead of one lifelong career.

When we asked survey respondents if they believed a person's calling lasts a lifetime, most people said no. In fact, nearly 70 percent don't view calling as a single, unchanging reality.[3] Today's leaders no longer see vocation as a life sentence, working in only one career with one organization for a lifetime. Your gifts and passions will often lead you to an area of work or a type of work, but you'll often find yourself shifting within that range. And that's okay. While this isn't an excuse to jump from project to project and run away from committing to a particular career path, it does allow us to relax, step back, and ease into the sweet spot that God has for each one of us.

Of course, there is a shadow side to calling, especially for those of us who consider ourselves type A leaders. Purpose, if left unbridled, can actually become a negative force in one's organization. It can smother team members, tear down healthy boundaries, and obliterate grace in the midst of failure. So we must learn to temper our sense of calling, aware that unchecked ambition can transform a person from a compelling leader into an ideologue. Passion can become obsession. A brisk pace forward can escalate into a full-speed-ahead run that barrels over people.

If this sounds like you, build better boundaries. Don't allow your ambitions to blind you to the team's needs, the organization's health, or the well-being of your family. If you're like me, you have a tendency to leave others in a ditch on the side of the road as you speed toward your goal. So give others permission to push back when you lunge forward. Find a mentor or peer who can make sure you temper your passions. Create accountability in your leadership style and a system that will force you to make quick adjustments when you lose your way, and give team members permission to speak freely and challenge you.

Never be afraid to charge a hill, overcome an obstacle, or maneuver around a hurdle that keeps you from achieving what you believe God is calling you to. But never let such pursuits destroy the people and systems you'll need to keep moving forward when the dust settles.

DEVELOP A CALLING STATEMENT

For five years, I was part of the team that produced *Life@ Work* magazine, a publication committed to wrestling through issues of faith and vocation. We had a definition of *calling* that formed the foundation of our work, and I still believe it to be better than most: "God's personal invitation for me to work on His agenda, using the talents I've been given in ways that are eternally significant." For some of us, the invitation just appears in our mailbox one day with our name on it. But for most of us, it takes time and prayer and a period of discerning.

Asking the right questions is crucial for discerning one's calling. Oftentimes, we fail to ask the correct questions and then wonder why our answers are so dissatisfying. Seeking God's will for your life begins by asking yourself, "What keeps me awake when I should be falling asleep at night?" The answer will expose what makes you mad, what makes you cry, what lingers in your mind when the world goes dark. The second question you should ask yourself is, "What wakes me up when I should still be sleeping in the morning?" The answer will uncover what you value, what you're committed to, and what excites you.

Asking questions like these is key to finding the right answers. Here are several others I think are helpful for deciphering God's invitation to you:

1. What are your passions and gifts? At the intersection of these two elements, you'll find your purpose in life.

2. What would you work on or want to do for free? That is usually a good sign of what God has designed you to do.

3. What energized you when you were a child? Does it still animate you? Knowing your calling is often directly connected to childhood passions and gifts.

4. If you could do anything and take a pay cut, what would that be? You may have to blow up your financial goals in order to pursue your true calling.

5. What barriers are preventing you from pursuing your true calling? Can you begin removing those?

6. If you aren't engaging your gifts and talents where you find yourself now, could you make changes in your current role to better engage those? Don't rule out the possibility that where you are is where you need to be.

When you've answered these questions, I suggest drafting a calling statement for your life. Remember to write in pencil, not ink, as it may change over time. My own calling statement reads, "To influence influencers through gathering, inspiring, connecting, and equipping them to become change makers."

Take the time to draft your own statement, because God has a unique purpose that He desires to carry out in you. It's your niche, your uniqueness, that specific and significant thing God has for you. Sure others will do similar work to yours, but they can't do it exactly like you. Why? Because you're the only you there is. Being a catalyst leader means you are working to identify, understand, and pursue God's unique call on your life with passion and patience. And once you locate that calling, guard it as a precious treasure.

> Higher calling matters. When you care so deeply about the why—why you're doing what you're doing—then and only then are you operating in a way that allows you to overcome the obstacles.
>
> —DAVE RAMSEY, AUTHOR AND RADIO HOST

In J. R. R. Tolkien's Lord of the Rings trilogy, we find Frodo wondering why he has been chosen to carry the magical ring on such a perilous journey. Like us, Frodo doubts that a meager man like himself could effectively carry out such a daunting task. "But you have been chosen," Gandalf says to Frodo. "And you must therefore use such strength and heart and wits as you have."[4]

Reflecting on this great line, author and pastor John Ortberg says, "This sense of having been called—the worthiness of it, the glorious goodness of a life lived beyond an individual's agenda—is a precious thing. It is sometimes subverted into grandiosity. It is perhaps more often lost in the ministry of the mundane. It needs to be guarded."[5]

As we locate the warm embers of God's calling inside ourselves, we must faithfully fan those flames. God desires for a sense of mission to burn within us, driving us forward in the perilous journey we call life. My high school graduation is a distant memory, but the spark of purpose I felt that day has continued to burn. I believe God has a unique purpose that He desires to carry out in every single person He creates. He's carved a specific and significant path for us all. This divine course is not mysterious or evasive, but walking it likely requires sacrifices. Yet you're guaranteed to gain much more than you forfeit.

FIVE CALLED LEADERS YOU SHOULD KNOW

- ## AUSTIN GUTWEIN | HOOPS OF HOPE

  After nine-year-old Austin watched a video about children who had lost their parents to AIDS, he felt called to do something. Today, Austin runs an organization that raises money through an annual basketball shoot-a-thon. Hoops of Hope has raised over $2.5 million to date.

- ## SHAUNA NIEQUIST | AUTHOR, SPEAKER, AND MOTHER

  Shauna is an amazing communicator (and also the daughter of Bill Hybels, so perhaps it runs in the genes) who focuses on balancing her calling as an author, speaker, and mother. She is the author of multiple books, such as *Cold Tangerines* (Zondervan, 2010) and *Bittersweet* (Zondervan, 2010), that have impacted many in the younger generation.

- ## BRYSON AND EMILY VOGELTANZ | DO SOMETHING NOW

  Bryson and Emily are committed to helping the next generation of leaders tackle many of the justice issues that are tearing apart our communities. Part of the Passion Conferences team, they desire to raise awareness and find solutions to issues of injustice.

- DANNY WUERFFEL | DESIRE STREET MINISTRIES

   You may know Danny as a national-championship-winning NCAA quarterback, but in recent years he's followed his calling to help the poor. His ministry equips leaders in impoverished communities to transform broken communities into desirable places to live.

- CHARLES JENKINS | FELLOWSHIP MISSIONARY BAPTIST CHURCH

   Fresh out of seminary at the age of 24, Charles was summoned into the office of his legendary eighty-year-old pastor. "Charles," the preacher said, "you're my man." Today, Charles pastors that historic church in Chicago. With a passion for helping the hurting and a burden for his city, Charles has made an eternal impact by living his calling.

2

AUTHENTIC

UNLEASH THE REAL YOU

Be yourself. Authenticity trumps cool every time.
—CRAIG GROESCHEL, CATALYST WEST

MY ASSISTANT, MICHELLE, HANDED ME MY MAIL AS SHE DOES each day, but this stack of letters looked different. Atop the pile was an envelope printed on ivory cardstock with gold trim.

"Looks like you got something official in the mail today," she commented, pointing to the embossed presidential seal.

I thanked her for the delivery before gently opening the envelope so as not to tear it. Inside was an invitation from the president to the White House Easter Prayer Breakfast with instructions on how to RSVP. The event was about a week away, but I immediately responded via e-mail with information required for security clearance.

When you get invited to the White House, you go.

I woke the following Monday flooded with insecurity. *Why do they want me at such a prestigious event?* I wondered. Despite my confusion, I packed my suitcase and headed to the Atlanta airport.

After checking into my hotel, I headed to the White House as the invitation instructed, still half expecting someone to call my cell phone to inform me that I'd been invited by mistake. As I walked to the entrance at the southeast corner of America's most famous home, I noticed a well-dressed couple waiting for assistance.

"Is this the check-in station for the prayer breakfast?" I asked them. "Yes it is," the man replied. The couple turned toward me and smiled, and I realized I was in line behind Joel and Victoria Osteen.

Having passed through White House security, which is far more invasive than airport TSA, I entered the side doors at the east entrance and stepped over a rug adorned with the presidential seal. Visiting the White House washes one with a sense of power and significance that's difficult to describe. Secret Service agents observe your every move. Interns and staffers rush from room to room. Portraits of past presidents dot the walls, interspersed with photographs of the current president and his family.

As I made my way to the East Room, I passed through

the walkway toward the lower basement level of the White House. I began to recognize rooms from news snippets and TV shows. A woman at a desk handed me a name badge and directed me up the stairs to the main entryway of the room where we were gathering. Uniformed military personnel stood at attention by the door, and melodies from an orchestra filled the air. A server offered me an orange juice on a silver tray. Quite a change from the miniature cartons and poke-through straws I was used to.

I walked down the main hall where great presidents had walked, entered the historic East Room, and found myself among a who's who of Christian leaders. Willow Creek pastor Bill Hybels stood to my left. Methodist megachurch pastor Kirbyjon Caldwell stood to my right, in deep conversation with Reverend Al Sharpton. Pastor Joel Hunter, a top spiritual adviser to President Obama, waved to me from across the room.

I was tempted to mingle with the impressive guests. But my grumbling stomach led me to a waiter with a tray of hors d'oeuvres. The most vivid memory I have of this event is the miniature sausage biscuits. They tasted like presidential food should, melting in my mouth. I wanted to stuff a few in my pocket to enjoy later, but I didn't want to be "that guy." I took two, thanked the server, and found my assigned seat.

The president arrived about thirty minutes later—fashionably late, as one might expect. He shook hands, slapped backs, laughed, and expertly worked the room. Joshua Dubois, executive director of the White House Office of Faith-Based and Neighborhood Partnerships, accompanied him. As they made their way toward my table, I attempted to plan what to say. Everyone else seemed to be spending their ten seconds with the commander-in-chief bragging on their accomplishments, and I didn't want to bomb. *Should I begin with "four score and seven years ago" or pull a lesser-known quote from a founding father from my iPhone?* I decided to be myself and shoot from the hip.

"Mr. President," Joshua said, "this is Brad Lomenick, who runs a community of young Christian leaders called Catalyst."

"Welcome, Brad," President Obama said. "I've heard good things about your work."

I said the first thing that came to mind: "Thank you, Mr. President. It's nice to meet you. By the way . . . nice jump shot."

I'm an avid sports enthusiast and remembered that just days before this event the president had sustained an injury while playing basketball.

The president laughed and smiled, perhaps refreshed by the lack of self-praise he'd received from many other guests.

"Nice to meet you, too, Brad."

As I've reflected on that exchange, I've realized a great lesson about leadership: I'm best when I'm being me. Every leader faces a temptation to project a persona rather than be themselves. They think that in order to maintain the confidence of their team, they must appear faultless, flaw-less, and ever wise. Yet most organizations need an authentic leader, not a perfect one.

I've often been tempted to pretend I'm someone else. When I arrived at Catalyst a decade ago, I was struck by how cool everyone seemed to be. The team produced sleek graphics and logos. Creativity flowed like a river, buffeted by a keen awareness of the day's trends. Likewise, the Catalyst community is noticeably innovative, hip, and dare I say, fashionable. Skinny jeans are ubiquitous at our events, but I'm more comfortable in khaki Carhartts. In fact, my legs are so fat that every pair of jeans I wear is skinny, but that's an entirely different matter. My V-necks reveal my Hanes undershirt—I'm sure a fashion no-no. Many participants spike or sweep their hair according to the latest styles, but I don't even have hair. In many ways, Catalyst is everything I'm not.

But our organization doesn't need a leader with cool hair and skinny jeans. They need someone they can trust and follow. That can only happen if I embrace who I am rather than try to be someone else.

Perhaps the ultimate freedom is the freedom to be one's self.
— DANIEL PINK, AUTHOR

If you've led for very long, you've likely experienced similar insecurities. Almost every leader I know fights this battle, struggling with feeling good enough or smart enough or relevant enough. Ambition beckons us to be the person we think everyone else wants us to be. That person is usually different than who we truly are. If we don't learn to be content with who God has made us and called us to be, then we will never reach our potential as influencers.

People are more perceptive than we give them credit for. They recognize when we're putting up a front or constructing a false persona. I've been around leaders who make awkward attempts at humor because they want to be perceived as funny when they're naturally serious. I know leaders who inject their vernacular with big words to sound intelligent when their true strength is an accessible earthiness. Usually, the leader is the only person who doesn't realize how uncomfortable they're making everyone else.

These urges typically come when we enter places where we feel we don't belong. When we find ourselves in a creative meeting, surrounded by people who are more innovative than us. Or when we're sitting at a table with individuals who seem more informed about current events than us. Or when we face off in a presentation against someone who seems more intelligent or capable than us. Or when we end up at a White House prayer breakfast with well-known pastors and Christian leaders, but deep down we know we're just good ol' boys from Oklahoma. When you find yourself in such situations and feel the urge to pretend you're someone else, resist it. The best person you can be in that moment is the one you already are.

NO FAKES

We live in a world of fakes. We fill our office buildings with plastic plants because we want the space to feel vibrant without having to do any upkeep. If we don't like the way our noses or eyelids or stomachs look, we can fix it with a call to a plastic surgeon. We airbrush models on magazine covers and Photoshop family portraits. And we even create online pseudopersonas through social media and blogs that project who we want people to think we are.

The digital age makes it easy to be inauthentic. Individuals now have the power to create a person in whatever image they choose, even if it doesn't match reality. The person who sends inspirational tweets or smiles in pictures on Facebook doesn't have to be the one who lives inside us. New media encourages us to be "on" all the time, and in such a setting, authenticity requires intentionality. Social media must be viewed not only as a way to connect but also an avenue for honesty about who we are.

There's beauty in imperfection. When something becomes too polished, it loses its soul. Authenticity trumps professionalism!

—CHRISTINE CAINE, COFOUNDER OF THE A21 CAMPAIGN

As unhealthy as modern media trends are, they have a positive side too. Authentic leaders rise to the top in a world of knockoffs, imitations, and counterfeits. Our society has created an appetite for authenticity. Consumers crave magazine covers without unrealistic, Photoshopped veneers. Documentaries center on raw backstage interviews and honest encounters. People demand musical artists who avoid lip-synching at concerts and award shows, as Ashley Simpson can attest. Today, authenticity is not just expected; it's required. Forty percent of respondents in our research said authenticity is one of the most important leadership traits of the next decade, and 47 percent said they first look for authenticity in a potential boss.

SHARE ON 🐦 📘
New media encourages us to be "on" all the time, and in such a setting, authenticity requires intentionality. #CatalystLeader

The journey begins with learning to be comfortable in your own skin. With looking at yourself in the mirror and saying to your reflection, "I'm okay with who I am. God made me this way for a reason." As leaders, we're expected to be the real deal.

I've had to take my own advice on more than one occasion. I'm not the best looking, most intelligent, or funniest person in any room. I drink way too much Diet Dr. Pepper and eat way too many Wheat Thins. I'm a decent communicator, but not a world-class speaker. I struggle with self-confidence, which can be both a burden and a blessing. It keeps me from feeling like I've arrived but sometimes prevents me from feeling like I belong. Like many others, I have a difficult time showing weakness and being vulnerable.

Most significantly, I long for friendships but struggle to invest in them. I'm more comfortable keeping people at arm's length versus letting them inside my life. As a result, I have lots of acquaintances but few true friends. One reason for this is that my career path has led me through many transitions, many of which required a long-distance move. I've grown accustomed to short-term relationships. Another reason is that my role at Catalyst means I have the ability to provide access to a large community. Anyone in a position like that knows this means everyone wants to be your "friend." Perhaps this is the burden of leading a large and visible organization. I've put up emotional walls to protect myself from getting used by everyone who wants something from me. As a result, I wrestle with being authentic and nurturing close friendships. I'm trying to tear down my walls brick by brick and build deeper relationships outside of work. I've had to work doubly hard at developing authenticity in my life. I have a sense that my responsibility as the leader of Catalyst is to have it all together. Sometimes I have to look at the imperfect reflection in my own mirror and, with cracker crumbs on my shirt, reaffirm my commitment to accepting myself.

Today's leaders must develop the art of self-awareness. We must grow comfortable with who we are before we can share that person with others. Recognizing one's true self is a prerequisite for releasing one's true self. No one wants to work for someone who seems unaware of his or her faults, failures, and weaknesses. But as pastor and author Mark Batterson says, authenticity is the new authority in leadership.[1] Sharing your failures and weaknesses is crucial to letting people in and empowering you to lead well. Those around you will connect with you more when they share in your failures and not only your successes. It's okay for those around you to see your weaknesses. We don't have to be perfect, but to be catalyst leaders, we'd better be authentic.

> Originality is overrated. Authenticity is what matters.
> —WHITNEY GEORGE, YOUTH PASTOR AND SPEAKER

After graduating high school, I was given the opportunity to travel with an Oklahoma all-star football team to New Zealand and Australia to play some exhibition games. I remember standing on the famed steps in front of the Sydney Opera House taking team pictures. There were lots of other tourists around, and we were creating attention. Because of our uniforms, a few of them assumed we were professional sports stars. They wanted to pose with us for pictures. Finally, one turned to me and in broken English asked, "Are you Joe Montana?" I paused. "Yes, I am!" This caused quite a craze for pictures, and someone in the world has a picture of me that they think is of one of the greatest quarterbacks in the history of NFL football.

Now, years later, I still fight the desire to be someone else, an improved version of my true self. I spoke with a well-known reporter recently who asked me to name aspects of my personal leadership style that I would change. "There's nothing I can think of," I responded. The answer was more than stupid; it was a flat-out lie. What I should have said is, "How much time do you have?" My life is full of frustrations and disappointments and failures, but I wanted her to think I had it all together. She knew my answer was inauthentic, and looking back, I recognize she would have respected me more if I had been honest.

Many leaders today feel great pressure to succeed, and as a result, create and accept a pseudoself. This is a version of them that hides their warts and magnifies their best traits. Unfortunately, those who know us best and even those who simply work with us every day see right through this. They recognize our true self and know we're not embracing that person. We won't reach our full potential by investing energy into creating false versions of ourselves.

Chris Seay helps emcee Catalyst events and leads Ecclesia Church in Houston. He recently challenged our speakers and band members at Catalyst events to make sure they hung out in the lobby, prayed with attendees, and avoided spending all their time in the green room. He told us, "The more ladder rungs you climb within an organization, and the more power you have access to, the more chance of being inaccessible and protected. Once you climb a rung on the ladder, the harder it is for you to come down. It's much harder to move down a notch on the ladder after going up. So be very careful how high you go on the untouchable ladder, because coming down hurts way more than going up."

For years, music artist Carlos Whittaker has put his life on display through his blog and honest writing, allowing thousands to be part of his Ragamuffin Soul community. He's shared openly about his struggles with an eating disorder and how he was able to overcome it through the support of his friends and God's grace. Carlos creates immediate trust with his blog community because he is vulnerable, approachable, honest, and real.

Carlos and many other friends of mine share openly about the steps they are taking to make sure they continue to stay healthy as leaders, including counseling, accountability, friends, and medical treatment. He reminds us that we are all on this journey together. None of us should be ashamed to reach out and ask for help.

Why Leaders Need a Confidant
http://catalystleader.com/confidant

My friend Vicky Beeching is a songwriter, worship leader, and now PhD student who also has been very authentic in dealing with a recent case of burnout, causing chemical imbalances that were dangerous and potentially life-threatening. She shared about her struggles in 2012 at Catalyst in Atlanta.

Michael Gungor is one of the most talented musicians out there. He and his wife, Lisa, decided to form a new band a couple of years ago after being in the Christian music scene for over a decade. When it comes to authenticity, many times one of the hardest things to do is return to your roots, especially in music. But they took the risk of forming a new band so they could share their true selves with the world and their fans.

Leaders like Carlos and Vicky and Michael aren't just called and capable; they are open and honest about who they are. We have to credit some portion of their success to this refreshing but often missing leadership trait of authenticity. Leaders who are willing to share honestly about their own struggles immediately gain influence.

A Lifetime of Leading Well: Chuck Swindoll

Chuck Swindoll has been a hero of mine for many years because of his authenticity. He has impacted millions around the world through his ministry—from penning books to pastoring a church to a far-reaching radio ministry. I remember working at Lost Valley Ranch and listening to his sermons on the radio as I drove to Colorado Springs on my day off. Though I may have begun the trip stressed or depressed, after listening to Chuck Swindoll's sermons, I arrived refreshed.

I talked to him for the first time several years ago to invite him to speak at our Catalyst Atlanta event. I was nervous when speaking to him over the phone—not because he was some sort of celebrity but because he has meant so much to me over the years.

From the first sentence he spoke, I was at ease. Swindoll is marked by an approachable, down-to-earth demeanor, and he wasn't afraid to laugh at himself. He mentioned that he was surprised by my call because he wasn't sure why I would want "some old guy" like him speaking at Catalyst. Unlike other leaders I've spoken with, this wasn't false humility. That's just who he is.

Upon meeting him in person at the event that year, my perceptions held true. He wasn't demanding or guarded; he was at ease with everyone he met. That day he spoke about how he had often failed in life, and he described his shortcomings in detail. He said that faithfulness is a key to being a great leader. He urged attendees to stand strong when others criticize them and to stand firm when everyone else may be moving in a different direction. When he finished, the crowd was clearly impacted. As was I. The man I had admired from afar for many years was the same up close as he was from a distance.

Authentic leaders have to be approachable and real. Over the years at Catalyst, we've tried to be authentic as an organization and as a leadership movement. We strive to be available, answering e-mails quickly, and even posting our e-mails on our website. We've maintained a concierge service since we started Catalyst that made following up with folks and connecting personally a priority. It's incredibly important to us that we are authentic, humble, and personable. No matter how big our organization gets, we want to maintain this essential trait.

I try my best to be personable, even as Catalyst continues to grow. When you are in a hurry or think someone isn't worth your time, remember that you were once in that position. One piece of advice I tell leaders all the time is when you're small, act big. And when you're big, act small.

SHARE ON 🐦 📘
Know who you are. If you try to be all things to everyone, then you'll end up being nothing to everyone. #CatalystLeader

Author and friend Bob Goff values authenticity and approachability. He even put his cell phone number in his recent book *Love Does*.[2] He wants folks to connect with him and feel the ability to talk with him. Accessibility is so important in today's culture. With social media and technology, the game has changed. People expect to be able to always connect with you.

Here are some best practices I've found helpful to cultivate the essential leadership trait of authenticity:

- *Practice self-awareness.* Before you can release your true self you have to recognize your true self. Too many people refuse to accept and even name their weaknesses, struggles, and pitfalls. As a result, they accept a version of themselves they believe others will like better. Understand who you really are.

- *Question yourself.* I encourage leaders to evaluate their self-acceptance with honest questions: Whose attention do you crave? Are you chasing the approval of friends, colleagues, and customers? What is it you don't like about yourself, and how can that short-coming also be a strength? Self-diagnosis can lead to self-discovery, which is the only path to authenticity.

- *Move from self-promotion to storytelling.* I can appreciate the effort made by individuals in the public eye to shape their personal brands. But I also worry about the effects this can have on living an authentic life. If you want to be a change maker, begin to see public outlets as places for sharing your personal story.

- *Resist the urge to create a digital alter ego.* Refuse to hide behind a website or Facebook page. Instead, adopt the mind-set of Claire Diaz Ortiz, social innovation director for Twitter: "Social media is not just about being connected. It's about being transparent, intimate, and honest."[3]

- *Learn to laugh at yourself.* Don't take yourself too seriously. Instead, grow comfortable enough with who you are to laugh and laugh often. When you are able to accept and even chuckle at your blunders and mess-ups, others will too. And this common experience will help you bond with them.

- *Build a support network.* Beware of the temptation to surround yourself with flatterers who only tell you what you want to hear. Keep honest people in your life that can help you stay grounded and keep from thinking you've arrived.
- *Be interested over interesting.* Be more concerned with listening instead of talking. Focus on others, not yourself.

Constantly turn over the rocks in your life and leadership. Uncover areas that need to be made clean. Big things are at stake. It's exhausting to keep up a fake persona. Learn to be honest. It's easier to impress people from a distance, so many leaders keep others at arm's length. For example, we often prefer digital interaction to life-on-life exchanges. This insulates us and prevents others from uncovering our weaknesses and flaws. But it also reduces our ability to influence others.

This is why I think it is a good idea to invite a direct report you trust to do a 360-degree review of you every now and then. It's uncomfortable but also helpful. As Rick Warren says, "You can't love people and influence them unless you are close to them. Up close means you can see my warts. You can impress people from a distance, but you can only *influence* them up close."[4]

This means being willing to hear things you don't like without getting defensive. Tough conversations will lead to deeper intimacy and trust, and they will help you embrace your true self. If you're like me, the thought of this rattles your cage and makes you sweat. Being ourselves is more uncomfortable and difficult than we'd like to admit. But the result of authenticity is freedom from fear, and this is a liberty that every leader needs to truly reach their potential.

> Be strong in grace. Your grace, your gift, your ability, who God's called you to be, just be yourself. . . . Don't be anybody else, don't compare yourself, just be you. If "you" is not everybody's cup of tea, then don't worry about it.
>
> —JUDAH SMITH, SENIOR PASTOR OF THE CITY CHURCH

Be who you are. When we attempt to be someone else, we allow fear to control our lives. Fear that others won't like us. Fear that others won't follow us. Fear that we won't be good enough. Unfortunately, the real you has to surface at some point. So inauthentic leaders often end up living a fractured life where their true selves are unleashed in private or only with certain individuals. And as we've seen too often in modern times, living a secret life is fraught with many dangers. In the new economy of leadership, authenticity rises to the top. You must unleash the real you.

One of the challenges in organizations today is creating space for leaders to admit and share their challenges. We need to create community where people can talk about the things they are dealing with without getting arrows in the back. Be willing to share your struggles.

> To me, the pastor or leader who is viewed as a normal person has an extreme advantage over the one who is viewed as the perfect spiritual leader. To demystify your pastoral role, you'll have to take some self-revealing risks.
>
> —CRAIG GROESCHEL, SENIOR PASTOR OF LIFECHURCH.TV

At a recent Catalyst event, we filled hundreds of balloons with helium and offered them to attendees outside of the venue. When someone took a balloon, they were handed a marker and challenged to write their greatest fears on the balloon's face. Some scribbled "insecurity" while others wrote "failure" or "lack of acceptance." Participants then released the balloons and watched them float away. The lesson: you have to admit your fears in order to accept who you are and grow into the leader you want to become.

As those latex bulbs floated into the stratosphere that day, I felt a sense of authenticity descend upon our attendees. I hoped we'd made them better leaders through this small act that helped them become a bit less fearful and a bit more authentic. My hope was that they would live better and, as a result, lead others better.

FIVE AUTHENTIC LEADERS YOU SHOULD KNOW

- ## KALYN HEMPHILL | MODEL

  You might think it strange that a model would make the list of authentic leaders, but Kalyn is more than a typical model. The *Project Runway* winner uses her platform to fight autism and create positive messages for aspiring models. The advice she offers on her website: "Treat others as you would want to be treated, and never compromise what you know is right."

- ## JUSTIN MAYO | RED EYE

  Through Red Eye, Justin has built a community that brings together the sons and daughters of the rich and famous. He constructs safe places where people can be themselves, where nobody cares who you are. Red Eye is an ambitious venture that exudes authenticity.

- ## TONY WOOD | MOMENT CHURCH

  Tony is founding pastor of Moment Church in Orange County. Tony's story is one of authenticity and willingness to talk about failures and bad decisions. He has built a church based on authenticity and revealing your deepest struggles, which is highly attractive to twenty-somethings.

- JEANNE STEVENS | SOUL CITY CHURCH

  Jeanne and her husband, Jarrett, were comfortably on staff at a metropolitan megachurch, but they knew they were meant for something else. At God's nudging, they left Atlanta to plant Soul City Church in Chicago. Visit Soul City and you'll soon realize that it is an authentic community born out of the vision of two authentic people.

- KOHL CRECELIUS | KROCHET KIDS

  Kohl is an avid sports enthusiast with a love for crocheting, and Krochet Kids is an authentic expression of who he is. The international organization employs Ugandans, teaches them the trade of crocheting, and sells their products to vendors around the world. I'm amazed by the authentic movement Kohl has created with little more than yarn and hooks.

3

PASSIONATE

LIVE IN PURSUIT OF GOD

> God's presence is all that matters. If we are connected to Him
> we will bear much fruit. Everything is dependent on Him.
> —FRANCIS CHAN, CATALYST ATLANTA

I WAS SIX YEARS OLD WHEN I FIRST ENCOUNTERED GOD. HE DIDN'T
speak to me in an audible voice like a neighbor calling from
across the street. It was more of an intuition, like the moment
you sense someone is behind you and turn around to see a
friend walking up. Maybe it was the sound of their footsteps
or breathing. Either way, something told you they were there.

My parents drove me to First Church of God in Bristow,
Oklahoma, that day like every other Sunday. They walked me
down the hallway to my Sunday school classroom where my

teacher, Bunny Baker, welcomed me with a smile. With the assistance of flannel boards and often-outdated curriculum, Bunny imparted Bible stories and the gospel to the early elementary school class each week.

She never pressured us to become Christians, but Bunny often shared her desire for us to one day give our lives to Jesus. Her loving lessons rescued me that day. As my six-year-old ears listened to her speak, I felt God's presence draw near. Suddenly, all the stories she had shared and all the explanations of who God was grew clear.

I trace the genesis of my spiritual journey to that moment, but two years later I made a conscious decision to follow Jesus. I was mostly a good kid, but I also knew that I'd never be able to overcome the bad parts without help. Even as a child, I remember dealing with the tension of trying to be good but having my sinful nature get the best of me. At eight, I fully committed my life to following Jesus.

My faith blossomed during my preteen years. I spent time reading the Bible each day, and even won the Bible Bowl in fifth and sixth grades. I attended church religiously. I joined a singing group called the Young Believers. My friends—Freddie, Alan, Robyn, and two Ambers—and I would stand in front of our congregation every few weeks to throw down some "People in a Box" or "Have a Little Talk with Jesus." It was epic.

In middle and high school, my youth pastor, Tom Hopkins, had a profound effect on me through his sermons at our Wednesday night Bible study. I began to see my relationship with God less as an accessory to my life and more as a central part of my identity. My faith began to define the decisions I made, the way I treated others, and the type of leader I wanted to become. Though I'd not fully grasped my vocational calling, I knew I should not, could not, and would not separate my career path from the passion for God that was growing inside of me.

When the time came to begin looking at colleges, I was naturally drawn to Christian colleges. I figured if I wanted to apply my love for God to my full-time job, I needed to go into the ministry. Though I didn't feel called to work in the church world, I wasn't going to let go of my commitment to live out my faith vocationally. A Christian college seemed like the most natural next step.

For months, I struggled with this decision. My mind was torn between what I believed I needed to do in order to follow Jesus and what I felt in my heart God was pushing me toward. One day, I woke up with a startling realization: I didn't need to become a minister to follow Jesus. The stress of the decision miraculously lifted off of my shoulders and I decided to attend the secular university I felt God was leading me to. Though I had accepted that the pastorate wasn't for me and didn't yet know where I'd end up, I felt confident that I could bring my faith to bear on any career.

FOLLOW CHRIST WHEREVER YOU ARE

As I've observed promising young Christian influencers across America, I've found that they are equally fervent about connecting their work with their spirituality. In fact, 31 percent of respondents to our survey believe that "passion for God" is one of the most essential leadership traits of the next decade. They know the importance of this trait, and they are bringing it to bear in almost every field imaginable. Whether they work in business or the arts, education or the social sector, media or the church world, they are tying their love for Jesus to the work they do. They want their faith to be central to their lives, not an afterthought. This generation of leaders desires for a passion for Jesus and a heart to serve Him to be fully and holistically connected to everything we do and everything we are.

The great reformer Martin Luther was once asked by a man how he should serve the Lord. "What is your work now?" Luther asked. The man replied, "I am a shoemaker." Luther said, "Then make a good shoe and sell it at a fair price."[1]

The man was surprised at the answer. Luther didn't tell him to save funds for seminary or to become a monk. He didn't even tell him to make Christian shoes with a "Jesus fish" stitched on the side. Instead, Luther recognized the spiritual value of the man's everyday job and encouraged him to glorify God by doing that work well.

Being a change maker means realizing that commitment to God and passion for following Jesus cannot be compartmentalized. It cannot be restricted to Sundays and sacred spaces. For the catalyst leader, Mondays through Fridays are holy days. Boardrooms are sacred spaces, and so are Hollywood studio lots, high-rise offices, and neighborhood coffee shops. Accounting can be a spiritual act; practicing medicine can be a spiritual act; working on an assembly line can be a spiritual act; teaching can be a spiritual act.

Just as I once believed that following Jesus necessarily meant seminary and pastoral ministry, so, too, you may nurture insecurities about your work. But don't be fooled. No matter where you work, your job can be an act of worship and service to God. That's why we determined early on that Catalyst would not be a conference only for pastors and church leaders. We want artists and politicians and teachers and entrepreneurs and corporate leaders to join our community. They, too, have a divine purpose for their lives.

The apostle Paul knew this essential well. In his letter to the Colossians, he says, "Whatever you do, work at it with all your heart, as working for the Lord, not for human masters" (Colossians 3:23 NIV). He recognized every day as an opportunity to display one's passion for Christ in whatever space he finds himself. Like Paul, the catalyst leader strives to connect passion for God to personal calling.

The way we live out our personal callings says a lot about how we see ourselves. It reveals whether we view ourselves as worshippers or ones who desire to be worshipped. If the latter, your life and work will be me-centered. If the former, it will orient vertically. A catalyst leader understands that the foundation of life and the source of true influence must be a deep love for God and desire to glorify Him.

Consider Lecrae, who continues to gain influence in the

hip-hop world and broader music industry. He's a respected artist who grounds his work in a contagious love for God. So much of his credibility with his peers is due to the passion he has for both his craft and his Creator.

> The pinnacle of your Christian experience should be when you
> take everything that you've learned on the pew of your church,
> and it's mattered on the pavement of your life's circumstances.
>
> —PRISCILLA SHIRER, AUTHOR AND BIBLE TEACHER

Or consider pastor David Platt of the Church at Brook Hills. When he began to explore the New Testament teachings a few years ago, he was overcome with the conviction that we must live passionately for God. Not in a sappy, Christian camp way but in a radical way. He downgraded his house, led his church in a campaign to give away more of their money, and now spends hours teaching the Word through regular weekend services, as well as their online "Secret Church" events. In my conversations with David, I have been deeply impacted by his commitment to Jesus and his boldness and vitality. He says, "We are tempted at every turn to lead out in a crowd a pleasing Christianity that promises people everything while costing people nothing . . . [but] God is more interested in the sanctity of his people than the success of our ministries."[2] His influence continues to expand as he ignites in others a passion to take the gospel to the nations.

Passion is infectious, so I try to fill our team's ranks with people who display this trait. I want to be around people with passion. You can tell when someone truly loves what they do and their heart and soul is in their work or the project they are leading. When your heart is in it, it's no longer a job. It becomes something freeing and beautiful.

What are you truly passionate about? What are some things you can do for days without tiring? I love to duck hunt. For me, my soul comes alive being in a duck blind in the middle of Arkansas flooded timber on a winter's morning watching the sun rise over the horizon. It's one of the most authentic worship environments for me. But I don't want to duck hunt all day long, every day. It's a joy in my life, but not my life's passion. Equipping leaders, however, is something altogether different. Even though I may tire of my job from time to time, I never grow weary in this passion.

A Lifetime of Leading Well: Eugene Peterson

Though he's penned more than a dozen books, Eugene Peterson is best known for *The Message* translation of the Bible. Bothered that a generation was coming of age who were not connecting with the Holy Scriptures, he composed this paraphrase translation in contemporary language. The result is a piece of art and literature that has sold more than 10 million copies worldwide.

Eugene Peterson's passion for God is evident from the moment you meet him. It's a quiet and subdued passion, yet unmistakable. Now well in his eighties, his voice is soft but raspy. His body is frail yet full of energy. Even in his old age, Eugene Peterson shows signs of Spirit-empowered life. My time with him was brief, but I felt God's presence each moment. Peterson's passion for living a life that pleases God seems like the only thing on his to-do list.

Every word he speaks is rich with the history of a life well lived and a God well served. We offered him the Catalyst Lifetime Achievement Award a few years ago and inscribed it with his mantra and title of one of his most popular books: *A Long Obedience in the Same Direction.* If more Christians today lived like him, there's no telling what the impact of our faith community might be.

Listen to the teachings of Francis Chan, Priscilla Shirer, or Matt Chandler, and you'll hear passionate pleas to love God more. Or read the writings of Margaret Feinberg, who grips readers with stories of encountering God's greatness and allowing those experiences to transform our lives. "When we passionately pursue God above all else, the tone and tenacity with which we live our lives changes. Holiness beckons. Divine expectation flourishes. Hope returns. Love abounds," Margaret says. "In response, we awaken, toss back the covers, climb out of bed, and drink in the fullness of life God intended for us. We live alert to the wonders all around us and within us that expand our desire to know God more."[3]

Your vitality is going to not be so determined by how you manage your time or what programs you implement but really your vitality and strength in leadership comes from your knowledge of Jesus Christ and how well you see him and what you actually believe about him.

—MATT CHANDLER, AUTHOR AND PASTOR OF THE VILLAGE CHURCH

The list of passionate leaders includes social activists like Jamie Tworkowski of To Write Love on Her Arms and Bethany Hoang of International Justice Mission; abolitionist and activist Zach Hunter, who fights slavery around the world and advocates for those who have no voice; and Julia Immonen, who recently rowed across the Atlantic Ocean to raise awareness on fighting human trafficking. Whether speaking, rapping, rhyming, writing, or serving, our passion for God simply can't be contained. And it shouldn't be.

Through Catalyst, I've witnessed a generation who is living life in pursuit of a God they can't get enough of. They crave His glory in what they do, and they are better leaders as a result. Their passion for God is contagious. If you are around them you can't help but be caught up in it.

Some culture watchers focus not on stories like these, but on the stats instead. Young people *are* leaving the church in record numbers. Yet I'm witnessing the passion of those who are choosing to stay. I see the twenty-thousand-plus who gather at Urbana every other year, the twenty thousand who gathered in Kansas City for the International House of Prayer's One Thing gathering, and the forty thousand college students at Passion Conferences. These events instill confidence that the next generation of leaders loves Jesus and is passionate about serving Him and making Him known among their generation. Not all of these worshippers are showing up at church on Sunday morning—at least, in this period of their lives—but their passion for God still burns strong.

Louie and Shelley Giglio of the Passion Movement have been shaping worshippers over the last two decades. They know a thing or two about what passion for God looks like. Louie describes a passionate church as being similar to a football game with a hundred thousand screaming fans:

> People show up with nothing to gain but want to be part of something bigger and give praise collectively to a team on the field. They scream, cheer, shout, and jump to help collectively raise the noise level. How much more should we do the same to bring praise to our King. King Jesus, who deserves a bigger sacrifice of praise?[4]

Christians today like to debate whether following Jesus with great passion is a matter of doing or being. But I think it is both. Following Jesus cannot be purely private. When God touches you, your passion for Him flows out of you and onto those around you through your actions. When God fills you up, like David, your cup will run over.

Your internal passion determines external reach. Your heart will shape the actions of your hands. For example, those who care *about* the poor will care *for* the poor. Active faith is becoming the norm for young leaders. They are integrating acts of justice, mercy, and evangelism into their work. They see both social justice and sharing the gospel as crucial to the advancement of the church and of God's kingdom.

SHARE ON 🐦 📘
Your internal passion determines external reach. Your heart will shape the actions of your hands. #CatalystLeader

As this new generation of leaders comes of age, they illustrate a pattern of passion, an unbroken call for letting love for God seep into all areas of life. As leaders who follow Christ and desire to become change makers, they inspire us to integrate this essential trait of passion both into *who* we are and *how* we pursue our personal callings.

GLORIFYING GOD

One of the biggest misconceptions about Catalyst is that we're solely a leadership development organization. While we want to develop our community's potential to impact and influence others, we also view ourselves as a spiritual development organization. Why? Because we believe there is and should be an intimate connection between the two.

Some Christians in the past have seen a firm dividing wall between the secular and the sacred. Their worship habits at church on Sunday were tangential to their work week. But this is not the way the world operates, and it is not the way following Jesus is designed to work. As God sparks the fires of our passion for Him, the flames engulf us. Everything we touch should bear the sooty fingerprints of our fiery zeal for Him.

Because of this, we hold Catalyst with open hands, not closed fists. If our organization disintegrates tomorrow, our team will accept it and move on. We believe this movement belongs to God for as long as He allows it to survive. Glorifying God is the heartbeat and soul of what we do.

Our team views spiritual stewardship as a part of our collective job description. Our financial success takes a backseat to our spiritual responsibility. This is not always easy. We're not a church. We're not a denomination. We're not a charity. But we are distinctly Christian, and with that commitment comes a belief that leaders' spiritual development is even more important than their professional development. So we carefully consider the spiritual components of our events. We could easily focus more on the head and not the heart, but we choose to give time to both.

We recognize that it is easy for people to attend a Catalyst event as pure entertainment or fun. So we've taken time to build in tangible spaces and activities to let people connect with God in their own way on a deeper level. We build in moments of quiet, moments of reflection, and moments of challenge. Catalyst is a space where we're as concerned about people's hearts as their heads and hands.

Every Catalyst event has included intentional times of worship, but several years ago we decided we wanted to push toward a more heartfelt perspective. Our team decided to focus on prayer since it is one of the best ways to fan the flame of spiritual passion. We can't live for God if we don't connect with God.

We started with an internal emphasis. Our team began to pray together after each Monday meeting. As our events approached, we began to ask God's blessings. On note cards, we distributed the names of band members, team members, and speakers. We prayed over these cards and over the programming, volunteers, and participants. We asked God to help us get out of the way so He could work in hearts. God began to move at each event, and we received stories from people who'd been impacted.

One e-mail that sticks out in my mind came from Bill who lives in the Southeast and works for a major airline. He'd been having an abysmal year financially, personally, and spiritually. He'd stopped attending church and moved away from his relationship with God. But when he attended Catalyst, everything changed. "Catalyst stabbed me through the heart," he wrote. "It made me realize what was important and that God hadn't abandoned me." As he found spiritual renewal, he began to grow as a leader.

Inspired by such stories of spiritual transformation, our team decided to push further. During our evening session a few years ago, Joel Houston and musicians from Hillsong NYC were leading worship, but we decided to add a time for participants to come out of their seats and pray with our volunteer team. I'll never forget the response. Standing on the floor of the arena, I looked upon crowds of people emptying out of their seats en route to the floor. People were weeping, crying out for God, and lifting their hands in worship. Others were putting their arms around them, laying hands on them, praying for them. I stood motionless at this sight, feeling that Catalyst was being spiritually defined.

We took the concept even further two years ago by adding a prayer tent at our events. Participants now had an open opportunity, rather than a scheduled one, to pray and to receive prayer. The tent became a place of profound life change. We received feedback from participants who decided to quit their jobs and fulfill what they believed was God's call on their lives. Others said they were freed from fears or feelings of unworthiness. Several decided to give up hidden sin in their lives.

As I read over these responses and encountered the stories of liberation, I was convinced that our conviction was correct. Passion for God was essential to leading well. Those who desire to influence and impact others will never reach their full potential unless they develop a contagious love for the One who has called them.

SEEKING GOD'S FACE

When you read the Scriptures, passion for God oozes out. Moses sought God every day. Job followed Him through the most devastating circumstances. Esther relied on Him at the risk of her own life. David chased after God, and his passion bleeds through the Psalms. The prophets craved hearing the voice of the Almighty, and the apostles joyfully followed Him to the grave.

These men and women were great leaders, yet modern influencers often overlook this trait. Too many build up their heads without minding their hearts. They read books on better business practices and attend marketing conferences, but spiritual development is often ignored. According to our research, only 11 percent of Christian leaders say "passion for God" is the leadership trait that best describes them. And yet my experiences with Christian leaders who are most success-ful today tell me that spiritual ardor is integral, rather than accessory, to leading well.

As Christians, spiritual passion has to begin with the Scriptures. God has spoken to His people through the Bible, and we must cling to His Word. We know that the Bible is a living, breathing book, not an outdated, stale tome. It provides timely truth about the God we serve and insight for how to live.

Many people today claim to love God but aren't rooted in God's Word and in their relationships with Him. If we desire to become passionate people in pursuit of our Maker, we must recover that. You may generate record profits this quarter and have great organizational victories, but if you aren't spiritually rooted, your life won't be as fruitful as it could be.

Francis Chan says,

> Time with God has to drive you. God's presence is all that matters. If we are connected to him we will bear much fruit. Everything is dependent on him. God is a real person. There is a real intimacy you can have with him. It's a real conversation when you pray and there are just times where you get away and say 'God, it's just you and me because you strengthen me like no one else can.' . . . Everything depends on my relationship with God.[5]

Do you spend time each week, perhaps each day, intentionally tuning yourself to God? Do you nurture a passion to see Him glorified in your family, relationships, and work, regardless of your vocation? I encourage leaders to set aside portions of their week to block out the pressures of life and pray, meditate, and seek God's face. Even if you are only able to set aside five minutes during the day to walk and pray, or simply read a few scriptures, you need to commit to this. These breaks will give you energy, enthusiasm, and renewed momentum.

Sustained leadership requires practicing the discipline

of replenishment. Pastor Bill Hybels says you need a strategy to accomplish this in your life daily, weekly, monthly, and yearly.[6] Leaders often get depleted by their work, and we need to recharge and regroup in intentional ways. Nothing will sap your passion for God like burnout.

One way to achieve this is to begin practicing the Sabbath. This means building margin into our lives. Margin is powerful and absolutely crucial for leaders. It allows for rest and rhythm to appropriately get played out in our routine. Margin is the fuel for responding to the unexpected and the option we all need for being more focused, intentional, and life-giving, and less stressed. Margin allows for rest, refocus, and adjustments as well as stirring our God-given passions.

I've noticed that as leaders' margins decrease, so does their spiritual vitality. But margins in business create profits; margins in family create memories; margins in personal finances create opportunities; and in all of life, margins create options to pursue dreams, pray, plan, and reflect. So create moments each week to practice the Sabbath. Building in times of rest will pay dividends.

Leaders are targets, so we all have to be grounded spiritually. Otherwise the pressures of leadership will get to you. We must continually grow in our faith and seek to know God more and more. Leaders must protect their hearts and constantly look for ways to grow and improve their inner lives, as well as their outer lives. The leader's heart is vital to being a change maker.

Passion for God makes us generous, active, and bold. If you're struggling to become a better leader, perhaps you should put down that sales book or take a break from those online videos on time management. Instead nurture your spiritual development first. Petition God to light a fire for His glory inside of you. Spend time in prayer and reflection and the Scriptures. Develop your heart for God and trust that He will help you lead well.

FIVE PASSIONATE LEADERS YOU SHOULD KNOW

- ZACH WILLIAMS | MUSICIAN AND WORSHIP LEADER

   Zach's lyrics are often spiritually evocative. His heart shines through in every note, and he is one of the most talented musicians and worship leaders I know. If you hear him sing or lead worship, you'll notice that he literally sweats passion.

- AMENA BROWN OWEN | SPOKEN WORD ARTIST

   Perhaps no one today delivers spoken-word poetry with passion like Amena. When she takes a stage, her love for God and pursuit of Him is readily apparent. When anyone talks about passion for God, her name always comes to my mind.

- PHILEENA HEUERTZ | WORD MADE FLESH

   When talking about passion for God, many think of crowds crying out for a divine touch in a packed arena. But Phileena has given that phrase new meaning by spreading a message of silence, solitude, and reflection. A revitalization is taking place around contemplative spirituality, in part because of her influence.

- PETE GREIG | 24-7 PRAYER INTERNATIONAL

   What Pete began in 1999 as a single night-and-day prayer vigil morphed into an interdenominational phenomenon. He is one of the founders of the 24-7 movement, and his Godward passion is so palpable that it's captured the attention of media from *Reader's Digest* to *Rolling Stone*.

- ## JAESON MA | MUSICIAN AND MINISTER

  Jaeson speaks to thousands of students around the world, challenging them to dive deeper in their love for Jesus. God is using Jaeson in amazing ways. He even prayed over Jeremy Lin the night before the now-famous athlete played his first basketball game with the New York Knicks.

4

CAPABLE

MAKE EXCELLENCE NONNEGOTIABLE

> Just keep taking the next step and keep having excellence in
> the ordinary.
>
> —DAVE RAMSEY, CATALYST ATLANTA

WHEN I WORKED AT LOST VALLEY RANCH FOLLOWING COLLEGE, I learned the meaning of hard work. And I learned it the hard way. My first day as head wrangler and ranch foreman, I committed to a standard and communicated that we would never compromise it: Lost Valley would be the cleanest and best-run guest ranch in the world. This was a lofty goal for a new foreman, especially when you consider that we boasted one hundred and fifty horses and two hundred cows. Not exactly an easy job.

My team members and I shoveled more horse manure than I care to admit. Because I'd been a ranch hand the year prior, I knew the importance of teamwork. I never asked them to complete a task I wasn't willing to do myself. On more than one occasion, I'd gather my team outside to clear the paths and roadways of equine excrement. The newbie ranch hands would always stare in shock when I'd come to join them, shovel in hand. My participation was an important symbol, demonstrating that no one was too important for the dirty work required to keep our ranch running.

"I know you may not feel like doing this work today, but we have committed to a standard of unwavering excellence," I'd say. "So grab a shovel, and let's make it happen."

As those last three words rolled off my tongue, our team would disperse for our messy but necessary tasks. The job usually took a couple of hours to complete each day, which is not surprising considering the amount of animals and acreage we maintained. Once we were done, the team would sit back, skin glistening with sweat and boots emanating with stench, to admire our success. Clean paths rested below the surrounding mountain peaks, and we all knew that our hard work and commitment to excellence was integral to making Lost Valley not just one of the most popular guest ranches in the world, but also the cleanest!

This excellence ethic was embedded into our organizational DNA. We were fiercely competitive, and everyone wanted to finish his or her assigned tasks before the others.

Our "hustle culture" caused us to run when others might walk, to always seek out the most difficult project; no one wanted to drive the tractor because that was considered the lazy man's job. We would fight over getting the least popular job or the most difficult assignment. This work ethic shapes me even today.

Of course, I wasn't always that way. I got my first job working at Reasor's Food Store as a stock boy. Every night, I was tasked with mopping the entire store. Time seemed to slow as my mop slid back and forth between shelves. I'd pray until I ran out of requests for God, and then I'd hum until I ran out of tunes.

The task was miserable, but the worst part of it was cleaning the produce section. When people step on dropped grapes, the stains are nearly impossible to remove. After a few weeks of straining my back to scrub them off the industrial tile, I began skipping an aisle every couple of nights. An older coworker who had been quietly noticing my bad habit finally pulled me aside and confronted me. "I know you've been skipping aisles, and I want to remind you that you're better than that," he said. His words gently shamed me, and I never skipped a row again. Maybe no one else would notice, but deep down I would know that I hadn't given my best.

Today, "make it happen" is one of my life's mottos because I know that a strong sense of vocational calling must match a high level of excellence. And for Christians, this is more than a matter of survival. It's a matter of stewardship. If we believe we are called by God to the work we do, then we bear the responsibility of doing this work with an unrivaled standard of excellence. We must strive for excellent work because we serve an excellent God. Rather than just punching a card or putting in our time, we're worshipping the One who gave us our talents by offering our best labor back to Him, regardless of profession or industry.

COMMIT YOURSELF TO EXCELLENCE

There are at least two components to leading capably: the right standard and the right staff. When I worked on *Life@ Work* magazine, our team determined that we would pursue excellence in every way. We sought expert voices, printed the magazine on high-quality paper, and utilized few or no advertisements. After several years, our circulation neared seventy-five thousand, but the number of subscribers hadn't risen enough to cover our costs. We were faced with a decision either to compromise the quality of our product or to go out of business. We chose the latter.

Anyone who has experienced a failure in their career knows how difficult the decision was. I was crushed. Every time I had to explain to friends that our publication had folded, it chipped away at my self-confidence. I felt like a loser and shouldered a tremendous amount of responsibility for what had transpired. Yet I still believe we made the right decision. Had we compromised our quality, the magazine might still be in business, but our staff would know we'd compromised something dear to us.

At Catalyst, we adopted the same rigorous commitment to excellence. We seek the best leaders in the world, regardless of their industry or beliefs. From Malcolm Gladwell to Jim Collins to Seth Godin to Tony Hawk, many great thinkers have graced our stage. It takes more work to put together this kind of program, but we believe it is worth the effort. We firmly believe in what Abraham Lincoln said long ago: "Whatever you are, be a good one."

As a team, we don't compare our events to other Christian conferences or even what some might classify as our "competition." Instead, we desire for our content, program, and production to be on the same level as TED or the World Business Forum or Davos. We want our production value to be akin to the Country Music Awards, Grammys, or a U2 concert.

SHARE ON 🐦 📘
Being a capable leader doesn't mean being big. Or being expensive. It's being excellent. #CatalystLeader

We also desire excellence in our customer service and the way we interact with our community—more Ritz Carlton than Howard Johnson. Through our concierge team, we attempt to combine professionalism with a personal touch. We have maintained the same value commitments we had as a team of three as the organization has grown through the years. The bigger Catalyst gets, the more we focus on realness, rawness, and approachability.

These commitments have also shaped our events. The rigorous process of planning a Catalyst event begins a year in advance and includes days of meetings, research, and brainstorming. We attempt to include surprising and memorable elements in every event. We've broken a world record at an event, raised millions of dollars for clean water, and even given thousands of participants drumsticks so we could make music together. When people experience a Catalyst event, we want them to walk away feeling like they've encountered a thoughtful, intentional, world-class gathering of young leaders unlike anything they'll experience anywhere else. We don't just want to do work that matters but work that sets us apart.

Everything from our marketing brochure to event websites to attendee notebooks and the Catalyst brand has always been designed with the highest standards. We knew early on that the best way to gain credibility was to create highly professional design and branding that was the best in the world. People are amazed, and probably annoyed, at how picky and detailed and unwilling to settle for anything other than excellence I am regarding our Catalyst brand.

Every great organization has a few areas where their standards are so high it's annoying. This is a good thing. Set standards that scare you, and work to achieve them. Know the areas you are so passionate about that you are willing to be uncompromising or even annoying. And remember that being a capable leader doesn't mean being big. Or being expensive. It's being excellent.

At Catalyst, we've grown very selective in regard to our print materials. We want our event notebooks, brochures, flyers, and curriculum to be done well. This doesn't just mean ensuring a consistent design with a high-quality look and feel. We also want to make sure our materials have been properly edited and contain captivating material. We know this is one of the first things participants encounter—and first impressions are only made once. We want those who attend a Catalyst event to get a sense of our high standards from the moment they encounter them.

Each year, we have brainstorming meetings where we invite creative people from outside our organization to join our team in dreaming about the next year's events. We first consider the needs of our participants—their struggles, concerns, expectations—and then we dream together. Nothing is too big, too outrageous, or out of bounds during these brainstorming sessions. The experience is always fun, but our team also carries a great weight of responsibility because we're acutely aware of our high standards.

We have a motto on our team that the best idea wins. And when it comes to ideas, we are ruthless. I've had an idea for an event theme for years that I've wanted to put into play—the word *kinetic*. I think it would make a great theme, and I push for it constantly. However, the rest of the team doesn't agree, and I've never been able to wield my authority or title for getting my idea through the system. The best idea wins, and we won't compromise.

If Cirque du Soleil ever comes to a town near you, make sure to purchase tickets. It will be one of the greatest leadership exercises you ever engage in. You'll learn about excellence, focus, teamwork, and many other qualities essential to organizational success. Many years ago, after attending a Cirque du Soleil performance, I read Lyn Heward and John Bacon's book, *The Spark*, which explains the details of the brainstorming process used by the Cirque du Soleil performance company. At Catalyst, we've incorporated many of the principles found in this book.

**How to Develop a Standard of Excellence
Based on Cirque du Soleil
http://catalystleader.com/cirque**

One fascinating story shared by Heward and Bacon is that the Cirque creative team often fights in their meetings. They defend their ideas through passionate arguments and intense debates. We've granted the same freedom in our Catalyst meetings, forcing ourselves to put our feelings on the shelf as we send out our ideas like knights to a joust. May the best idea win and all others die a hero's death.

If you walked into our creative team meetings without warning, you might think you'd walked into a bar brawl or a family reunion gone awry. Like other guests we've invited into the process, you'd likely feel uncomfortable at first. Faces turn red and voices raise as team members argue for their proposals. You might even assume we don't like each other much, but you'd be wrong. We have simply died to our egos for the sake of the creative process. Over the years, we've grown to like the tension, trusting that it often produces better ideas. And great ideas are exactly what we're after.

> God is an excellent God. He does things as well as possible. So should we. We want to do things the best we can do it, because God deserves our very best. God living in us informs the way we do things and the kind of excellence that God demands.
>
> — SHELLEY GIGLIO, COFOUNDER OF THE PASSION MOVEMENT AND SIXSTEPSRECORDS

We select our event themes about a year in advance, which is a difficult decision. One year we chose "Reverb" to communicate that what you create has a lasting effect and doesn't go away. Another year, we selected "The Tension Is Good" and set out to encourage participants to embrace the natural tensions that come with leading a team. For our tenth-year anniversary, we chose "Make Your Mark" to remind participants that leaders leave a mark wherever they go, and we should be intentional about our impact.

Selecting the theme is only the beginning. With our high standard in mind, we have to plan all the elements that go with it. Once we settle on what we hope to accomplish, the butterflies hatch. There's a healthy level of anxiety that the idea might not come off as well as we envisioned. Additionally, we've created a high expectation for creativity over the years—which is both a burden and a blessing. We want to delight our participants and don't want events to feel stale, so we have to push ourselves to meet our standard.

Our high standards at Catalyst require both a high level of quality and a high level of action. As entrepreneur Henry Ford famously stated, "You can't build a reputation on what you are going to do." Our big dreams must be accompanied by nearly flawless execution from each team member. We have a culture of action and excellence, bent toward making things happen. We have a small team, so the margin for error is razor thin. We have to be highly responsive and heavily committed to working until a job is complete. Our finish lines must match our starting points in scale, creativity, and excellence.

Before our "The Tension Is Good" event, I told my team early on that at the end of the program, I wanted to go out with a bang. The week before our event, we realized we hadn't secured anything to meet this goal. We searched tirelessly before we determined to shoot a man out of a cannon inside the arena. The budget was maxed out, but we didn't have anything else that would set this conference apart from other years. We made the call to move forward.

Because of our lighting rig, the stuntman had a difficult flight path. He had to fly over one truss and under another.

When the cannon fired, the tension we'd been addressing throughout the conference hung in the arena and people held their breath. He landed safely, and we all knew that we'd been successful in creating and achieving a standard that would scare most teams.

At our Atlanta "Make Your Mark" event, a man called Professor Splash jumped off a thirty-four-foot platform and belly flopped into a kiddie pool with only inches of water. We didn't know how we were going to build or rig the pool, and it sprung a leak during the previous session and needed to be repaired during the break. We weren't able to test the act beforehand—and even more troubling, we discovered that the good professor was attempting to break his own world record.

I remember sitting backstage a few minutes before the jump. Our team was eating lunch when one person asked, "What if he dies?" We all paused before rushing to locate an ambulance and sketch escape routes for the daredevil's body. But no amount of fear would hold us back, because we were committed to creating a significant moment that participants would never forget.

Our team held our breath as we watched Professor Splash jump. Thankfully, he hit his mark. And in a small way, we felt like we did too.

Holly Green, a writer for *Forbes*, says excellence is built on three pillars: clarity, focus, and, connection. Looking back on experiences like Professor Splash's belly flop, I see how each of these elements was necessary to achieving the high standard we had set.

"Excellence starts with getting very clear on the end state you wish to achieve (winning) and relentlessly driving towards it every day," writes Green. "Excellence requires knowing when to push on (even when you don't have all the information or the perfect solution), but doing it well and constantly refining as you forge ahead. Excellence means accepting only the best, and understanding that when it is not given that you, as the leader, are at least partly responsible."[1]

HIRE EXCELLENT PEOPLE

In addition to the right standard, a capable leader needs the right staff. Thirty-one percent of respondents in our survey said that competence was one of the most important leadership traits of the next decade, and they're right. That's why when I need to fill an opening on our team, I look for make-it-happen kind of people. They must be spiritually grounded and passionate about our vision. But a potential team member must also possess an ability to execute on a moment's notice.

As I mentioned in chapter 1, I worked for John Maxwell for several years at the leadership organization he founded,

INJOY. I traveled some with John and saw up-close his commitment to excellence. John Maxwell is a make-it-happen leader. Other staff members and I used to kid him for working during a plane ride while the rest of us were sleeping. He'd prop his feet up and edit books with his glasses resting on the tip of his nose. John would slip the manuscript in his briefcase when he disembarked the plane, but it would come back out when he got into the car. There was never downtime with John. Whether on a plane or in a car or sitting in a green room waiting to speak, John was pushing ideas and projects forward.

John has spent lots of time with many great leaders. And he would say that the one thing he's always noticed about the best leaders is that they have the ability to "make it happen" and get something over the finish line. When given an assignment, they deliver. Jack Welch calls it "getting out of the pile." Every once in a while someone sticks his or her head above the pile and gets noticed. This person takes the same job everyone else takes but actually delivers. In my own work, I've recognized that this characteristic separates good leaders from exceptional ones. When I surround myself with capable leaders, I'm free to "make it happen" with my own projects.

7 Leadership Lessons I Learned from John Maxwell
http://catalystleader.com/johnmaxwell

I look for team members who won't balk at difficult assignments and are willing to do whatever it takes to execute. This might be the number one trait I look for in potential hires. If a person is adept in taking an assignment—no matter how seemingly insignificant the task may be—and driving it to completion, they are indispensable. Catalyst's credibility is built because of hundreds of "small assignments" being done well and on time. The Bible offers much wisdom when it reminds us that people who are faithful with a little are also faithful with much (Luke 16:10).

Everyone on the Catalyst team needs to be a finisher. No one gets to simply be the "idea guy." Our team takes pride not only in creating concepts but also in making them reality. This is a distinctive part of our organization's culture. It's part of our DNA that has served us well. Too often, organizations get tied up in meetings trying to figure out who should be responsible for a project. An awkward silence fills the room until someone sheepishly raises his or her hand and assumes the role. What these organizations often need instead of another meeting is to develop a culture in which team members fight over taking the ball and running with it.

Why You Should Adopt a "No Meetings" Policy
http://catalystleader.com/nomeetingspolicy

Athletes understand the power of "making it happen." Sports teams thrive on those who deliver. At a recent Catalyst event, Miles Austin and Tony Romo from the Dallas Cowboys joined us. Miles mentioned that he was taught growing up to always choose the job no one else wants. Tony added the philosophy of "it's in the dirt." They know the power of hard work and discipline, and it's no coincidence that they are world-class athletes today.

Here are some marks I consider essential to being a capable leader:

- *Capable leaders constantly push forward.* Surround yourself with people who spend more time dreaming about tomorrow's possibilities than dwelling on yesterday's failures. It's easy to lament bad decisions, but a leader who can push ahead of them is invaluable.

- *Capable leaders are team players.* At Catalyst, we argue on principles, but we always have each other's backs. In order to succeed, you need confidence. And you can't have confidence without trust.

- *Capable leaders own their mistakes.* A leader who blames others for his mistakes cannot grow in his role. Look for team members who can admit missteps without growing discouraged.

- *Capable leaders are willing to take risks.* If an organization is going to thrive, the leaders must be willing to pioneer new territory. Surrounding yourself with people who will boldly step out even when it doesn't make sense is important.

- *Capable leaders are constant learners.* Capable leaders never stop growing and getting better. Learners are committed and coachable, always students and desperate to learn. They nurture a professional curiosity. What kinds of books are they reading, if any? Do they subscribe to any podcasts? How are they attempting to become better at what they do? Do they listen more or talk more? As your organization grows, you need team members who are constantly learning.

- *Capable leaders aren't entitled.* I believe that experience creates expertise. So the best leaders develop in the midst of action—doing, not just thinking or dreaming or talking. I need to know that my team is willing to break a sweat alongside me.

- *Capable leaders are anticipators.* You must stay a step ahead of the people you serve. Otherwise, you'll end up spending all your time reacting to problems and concerns and mishaps. It's imperative for leaders to figure out what the organization needs before anyone else ever realizes it.

- *Capable leaders are persistent.* They see things through and don't give up. They don't ask just once and read Facebook until they get a response. They follow up again and again until they get the answer or solution they need.

- *Capable leaders are trustworthy.* Because they can be trusted, capable team members are among the most valuable employees in any organization. When they make a promise, you don't have to worry about follow-up.

• *Capable leaders deliver.* Capable leaders get things done. I look for people who do what they say they will do. This allows me to delegate more and manage less. Team members need to make it happen no matter how insignificant the task or assignment.

I'm blessed to be surrounded by a team that meets these criteria and amplifies our organization's success. Leaders too often overvalue themselves and undervalue their teams, but the quality of one's team is as important—often more important—than the quality of the leader himself or herself. The right staff will carry you over the finish line when you might otherwise fall by the wayside.

A few years ago, Catalyst was producing two events each year. Our team decided that we had an opportunity to grow the organization. We made a bold decision to jump to eight events the next year. We weren't able to add any staff, so we were forced to produce four times the number of events with the same number of team members. Looking back, we bit off more than we could chew. But because we had the right staff committed to the right standards, we soared to success.

Many nights we worked until three or four o'clock in the morning, got forty-five minutes of sleep, and came back the next day ready to keep pushing. My team often pulled all-nighters before an event tweaking fonts and slides and program schedules, along with setting up bookshelves or creating artistic displays.

Hard work is a prison cell only if the work has no meaning.
—MALCOLM GLADWELL, AUTHOR

At our Dallas event that year, our notebooks failed to arrive. I panicked, but our staff began working to solve the problem. A team member in Atlanta rushed to Office Depot and printed new notebooks at a high premium, shipping twelve hundred of them through Delta Dash at three in the morning. Another team member picked up the books in Dallas at six, only a few hours before the event began. Our participants had no idea what we had to do in order to give them the experience they expected from us, but our droopy-eyed staff did. When the conference started, we handed out notebooks with a knowledge that we'd executed well. We had committed to make it happen even if it cost us more money than we thought or required more work than we expected.

How to Create a "Make It Happen" Team Culture
http://catalystleader.com/makeithappen

Capable leaders are willing to set standards that scare them. Ask yourself the question, "Are you operating at good, better, or best?" *Good* is doing what is expected of you. It is slightly above average and requires some focus and determination to get there, but is relatively easy to achieve. *Better* is rising a little higher than good. It typically means you are comparing yourself to the next one in line. But *best* is where you want to live. It is greatness and doesn't mean you are better than everyone else but that you're working to your maximum capability. It's about confidence, not arrogance. This is a standard unto itself. Walt Disney once famously stated, "Do what you do so well that they [your guests or clients] will want to see it again and bring their friends." So true. Excellence is nonnegotiable. Leaders should strive to be the best in the world at what they do. I believe God demands our best, and this is what I expect from our team and from myself.

Creating world-class events is not a science. No one has written an ironclad handbook on how to do it, and if they ever do, it will be outdated in six months. Each event needs to feel fresh, so once a program is implemented it cannot be duplicated. As a result, we've committed to building a team of capable, creative people who can feel their way through the process without losing their way. But believe me, I am constantly aware that I am not smart enough to deliver on the standard I've set for myself and the standard we've tried to maintain at Catalyst. I know it's a stretch and really difficult to maintain. We feel like we have to consistently outdo ourselves, but I love the accountability it creates for us to reach a new standard of excellence at every turn.

Likewise, no one has created a foolproof manual for the work you are engaged in. Resist the temptation to believe that you can carry an entire organization on the back of your talents or passions alone. You must surround yourself with equally gifted leaders who share a common commitment to excellence. Without this critical component, you will not be able to lead well.

EXCELLENCE BEGINS WITH YOU

A high standard of excellence starts with you. The most successful leaders of this generation recognize the value of excellence in their work. You may not know Joel Houston's name, but as the front man for the band Hillsong United and global creative director for Hillsong Church, he is someone who lives out the principles of being capable and demonstrating competence. If you've ever been to a Hillsong concert or visited their website, you've experienced their unflinching commitment to consistent quality.

As I've gotten to know Joel during the past few years, I've recognized the high standard of work he and his team pursue. They've avoided the pitfall of resting on their accomplishments or hitting the organizational cruise control button. Instead, they're always asking how they can be better and do better and lead more people into authentic encounters with God.

"Excellence is a spirit, rather than a presentation. But if

the spirit is there for excellence, then a great presentation will follow," Joel mentioned to me backstage at our Catalyst event in Atlanta. "Excellence starts with attitude and a servant's heart. Lift the standard always and be relentless in the pursuit of perfection, but excellence ultimately rises and falls on the spirit of your people, and spirit starts with you as the leader."

Joel says he must do two things to maintain excellence. First, he leads by example. A team can't follow a leader who isn't living up to the standards he's set for everyone else. Second, he values his people. People will only meet high standards if they feel valued by the standard-setter. If they are undervalued, they will underperform. But when they feel that their leader is on the journey with them and applauds their efforts along the way, they'll deliver excellence.

> If what you are doing is important, you will encounter resistance. If what you are doing isn't important, it will be easy.
>
> —DONALD MILLER, AUTHOR

Because of his team's hard work and God's grace, a little-known Australian church has risen to global influence. They've planted churches in the UK, Ukraine, South Africa, Sweden, and New York City. They also hold services in Paris, Konstanz, and Moscow. Hillsong has sold more than 12 million worship albums worldwide.

Like Joel, pastor Perry Noble is not one to hold back on challenging leaders. I love what he has to say about the church's commandment and commission toward excellence:

> The church is the bride of Christ—established by Him, purchased by Him and pursued by Him! We have the promises of God and have been empowered by His Holy Spirit. We should be doing things better than Apple, better than Disney and better than Google! There is way more at stake with what God has called us to! And "Spirit Filled" should not equal poorly planned, thrown together and poorly executed! And . . . no one should say, "I'm doing this for Jesus" and then follow it up with a half-hearted, underwhelming effort. When it came to redeeming mankind, Jesus did not search the back corners of heaven to find some under-challenged angel who had nothing to do . . . he came, he did it, he paid for the sin of the world!!! He gave his best, and His followers should do the same![2]

What these leaders illustrate is a renewed commitment among this generation to producing quality work and maintaining a high standard. As Scott Belsky argues in *Making Ideas Happen*, you have to create a system designed to help you execute and define what excellence means for your organization. Many leaders have not done either of these things, and as a result, they end up losing momentum, lacking passion for their work, and walking away from their calling altogether. Scott is inspiring a whole new generation of leaders to make it happen through the Behance Network, the 99% Conference, and the Action Method.

A Lifetime of Leading Well: Nancy Ortberg

Christian ministry is often a difficult place for talented and called women. But Nancy Ortberg has overcome many of modern ministry's obstacles by being exceptionally talented. Those who know her will tell you that she's a hard worker, quick thinker, and rigorously committed to excellence.

Nancy has worn many hats throughout her life, but she's never failed to succeed. She has successfully worked in sales, healthcare, leadership development, and ministry. She served for eight years as a teaching pastor at Willow Creek Community Church, one of America's largest congregations. The books she's authored include *Looking for God: An Unexpected Journey through Tattoos, Tofu, and Pronouns* (Tyndale, 2008) and *Unleashing the Power of Rubber Bands: Lessons in Non-Linear Leadership* (Tyndale, 2008). Nancy does leadership consulting these days while helping oversee Menlo Park Presbyterian Church with her husband, John. And she's raised three amazing children to boot.

Having known Nancy for many years, I admire her ability to improve her leadership skills with time. She never stops looking for ways to get better at what she does. She has a relentless drive for improvement. As a result, she has influenced leaders all over the world and has launched multiple ministries and business ventures. She carries credibility among top-level leaders in both the business community and the church. This is a difficult balance, and one she does with grace and respect. Nancy's proven record of excellence in every season and aspect of her career is an example of how capability can propel a leader forward.

In speaking of her work, she gives insight into how she's able to get things done and accomplish much on a constant basis:

> Leadership becomes about activating your team, collaborating, and allowing everybody to have room at the table. . . . I had a boss tell me once that 70 percent of leadership is perseverance, and I thought that was the most unprofound advice I'd ever gotten. Today, I think it's incredibly wise. It's not stupid perseverance, but it's that leadership is not about being famous, but it is really hard work. And if you don't want that, don't sign up for it.[3]

GOING ABOVE AND BEYOND

If you are pursuing your calling but feel as though you fail to achieve high standards, I've got good news for you: excellence is an essential anyone can express. We can all push through the quitting points, making sure we give our best. We can all get dirt under our fingernails, hire a competent staff, and set a high standard. You must begin creating a capable culture. Once those two things are in place, the only thing left is to appropriately channel your momentum.

Capable leaders hustle. You have to be willing to work harder than anyone else, stay late, arrive early, start new projects, learn more, make it better, take out the trash, stand on the stage, accomplish the menial tasks, create the vision, push yourself lower while pushing others higher. Capable leaders are not afraid to get their hands dirty and reach down into the mess to move things forward. Dirt on your hands and sweat on your brow goes a long way.

> Whatever you are, be a good one.
> —ABRAHAM LINCOLN

One way to increase your organization's capability is to reduce sideways energy. This is the unnecessary force we often waste time and resources exerting that could be spent elsewhere. Sideways energy is exerted with an employee who has three sales to close but doesn't call them back because she's been asked to help clean up the office for the Christmas party. Sideways energy is generated when you spend hours creating a staff handbook that ends up collecting dust. Sideways energy is a company-wide system that forces team members to run the gauntlet of bureaucracy. Sideways energy is dealing with the same problem multiple times, or spending two hours talking about what you should have done an hour and a half ago.

One of my leadership landmines is micromanaging. I grow concerned with the status of assigned tasks—especially with the design of our brochures and marketing materials—and that can lead me to ask for constant updates. Not only can this communicate a lack of trust in my team, but it can create sideways energy. It forces someone to stop what they are doing to brief me on a project's status when that same time could be spent on completing the task itself. I've begun to realize that my tendency to micromanage my team undermines my desire for efficient, high-quality work.

Once we discover our calling, we have a responsibility to pursue that calling with authenticity, passion, vigor, and distinction. If we fail to set the right standard, surround ourselves with the right staff, and channel momentum properly, we'll underachieve. But even worse, we won't be honoring God by giving Him our best. Being the best requires focus, determination, intentionality, hard work, perseverance, risk-taking, and making sacrifices. The stakes are high. And we all know when our performance is not our best. Our families know it. Our friends know it. Our staffs know it. Our bosses know it. And God knows it. Make sure your standard is not just being better than average, or merely being better than your competitor. You must always strive to be the best you can be. Without a standard of excellence in your work, you have no hope for becoming a true change maker.

SIX CAPABLE LEADERS YOU SHOULD KNOW

- ## JENNI CATRON | CROSS POINT CHURCH

  As executive director of Cross Point, Jenni has earned a reputation as a gifted leader who improves every project she touches. Alongside pastor Pete Wilson, she's grown an incredible multisite congregation around Nashville. In a vocation in which women often struggle to garner respect, she's earned it through hard work and raw talent.

- ## JEFF SLOBOTSKI | BIG OMAHA

  Having helped run events myself, I know when events aren't produced well. Through Big Omaha, Jeff sets a standard for event excellence. His Nebraska event is a gathering place where young entrepreneurs and innovators can listen to presentations from the world's best and brightest thought leaders.

- ## BRANDON MCCORMICK | WHITESTONE MOTION PICTURES

  Brandon founded Whitestone to produce high-quality films with uplifting storylines. He and his team have produced award-winning short features and musical narratives that continue to delight audiences.

- ## JEREMY COWART | PHOTOGRAPHER

  Jeremy started doing photography out of his love for art, but he's been carried to the top ranks of his field through excellent photographs. He is known for his gifted ability to select optimal lighting and locations, and he has created breathtaking portraits of some of the most well-known celebrities in America.

- TYLER MERRICK | PROJECT 7

    Everyone seems to be launching cause-oriented businesses these days, but Tyler has created something extraordinary in Project 7. They sell high-quality goods and donate to worthy nonprofits that address seven areas of needs, including feeding the hungry, healing the sick, housing the homeless, and caring for creation.

- JULIA IMMONEN | ROW FOR FREEDOM

    Julia is the only person I know who has rowed across the Atlantic Ocean, all to raise awareness around the issue of human trafficking. She is an advocate with the A21 Campaign and also works with Sky Sports in London, as well as launching her own organization, Sport for Freedom, which takes on major sport endeavors to raise awareness for justice.

5

COURAGEOUS

PREPARE TO JUMP

> A single act of courage is often the tipping point for
> extraordinary change.
> —ANDY STANLEY, CATALYST WEST

STANDING ON THE TOWERING CLIFF LOOKING DOWN ON THE
frigid Canadian waters, my knees began to knock. My inner
conqueror was willing me to jump, but my inner coward was
begging me to stay. In a moment, my mind flashed back to
the journey that brought me to this overlook.

I'd met Bob Goff at one of our Catalyst events in which
we'd invited him to speak. The flurry of the gathering pre-
vented me from getting to know him or even having a decent
conversation. But I'd picked up on how authentic he was from
his bio and what others had told me about him.

Bob is known for his extreme optimism and willingness to find "capers." This term was Bob-speak for purposeful adventures. He is a lawyer who offices on Tom Sawyer Island at Disneyland in California. He wooed his wife by slipping PB&J sandwiches under her windshield wipers each morning. Bob took his children on a world tour to meet prime ministers and presidents, became a consul for Uganda, and has pulled off many amazing practical jokes. With humor and brass, Bob has pursued God's kingdom in mind-boggling ways.

He turned to me at our event and commented, "Hey, you should come out to our house. It's near Malibu." I was interested in what he was doing, so I decided to take him up on his offer. A free vacation in one of California's most posh neighborhoods didn't seem like a bad idea. Only later did I realize that he was referring to the Malibu camp in the middle of the wilderness of British Columbia, northwest of Vancouver.

I began to get nervous when my plane landed in Seattle and Bob told me we needed to get in a seaplane for the second leg of the trip. No pilot necessary—Bob would fly us.

The plane ride was tense, and I was filled with curiosity about what this visit would hold. To force my mind on other things, I stared out the window at the wilderness below. The landscape looked like Narnia. Snow-kissed mountains rose out of the sea on both sides. Waterfalls gushed from cracks in the rocks and splashed into dark-blue ocean. Low-lying clouds hovered beside the peaks as if to watch over the landscape. This was the most beautiful place I'd ever laid eyes on.

Breaking the silence, Bob pointed to his house. In the distance I saw a beautiful log cabin tucked into the side of a mountain peak. I realized why we traveled by seaplane: it was the only way. There was no road access to the house.

After we landed, I followed Bob to his house, where we unpacked and cleaned up. For the next four days, we relaxed, wrote, and hiked. If things got too quiet, Bob would jump up and insist we do something more exciting, like race four-wheelers or shoot guns.

The last day arrived, and I could tell Bob had something mischievous up his sleeve. He invited me to take a ride in his boat before we departed. Ten minutes of cutting through waves later, we arrived at a quiet place. I followed him up a narrow trail to the top of a steep bluff.

"I hate to spring this on you now," he said. "But you can't go back to my house, and you can't go home until we've jumped off this cliff."

I inched to the edge of the cliff and stared down what appeared to be a forty-foot drop. The cold wind was whipping, and I knew the water couldn't be more than forty degrees. Yet I knew that if I didn't jump, Bob was just crazy enough to leave me there. I took a dozen steps back from the edge, stripped down to the bare minimum, and began to sprint for the edge. The energy from my fears turned into liquid courage.

When my feet pushed off the end of the bluff, I found myself in what seemed like another dimension. Time slowed for a moment and I considered the insanity of such an act.

My body adjusted for free fall and I let out an unstoppable yell. Then, as if time reset, everything began to move at a normal pace again. In an instant, I plunged into the frigid sea. I felt like I was jumping into the knife drawer. Flush with adrenaline and faintly hearing Bob's celebratory cries behind me, I swam back to the boat.

For the next thirty minutes, Bob and I discussed the exhilaration of that act. I couldn't believe what I'd done, but he said he never doubted I would. We had experienced a caper together. And in the slow-motion free fall into the Canadian sea, I'd discovered the secret to Bob's infectious lifestyle and leadership: courage. Bob's advice to me in parting that day was, "Live a courageous life that someone else would want to take notes on."

Without courage, your calling is crippled. Even if you have a crystal-clear vision from God about the path you should pursue—and most of us don't—it will not alter your direction one whit until you have enough courage to act on it. Courage moves us from ideals to action, from potential to actuality.

Like Bob, young leaders who are making an impact today are the ones who are taking risks, confronting evils, and rushing into dangerous places. Courageous leaders are working in their sweet spot but may be outside their comfort zones. And in their seemingly reckless attempts to live out their callings, they are becoming the kinds of leaders others want to follow.

TAKE HEART

Standing atop the overlook that day, I remembered something Tad Agoglia, founder of the First Response Team of America, said at Catalyst Atlanta: "Being fearless is less about operating with no fear and more about seeing the fear—and stepping forth in a grand effort to overcome."[1] Courage is not the absence of fear but rather the commitment to overcome it. Courage doesn't mean you're not afraid; it means you battle against your fear and confront it. Courage pushes you to resist the impulse to shy away from the things that stir up your innermost anxieties. Courage is required and must be a constant. It's tiny pieces of fear all glued together.

> Courage is not the absence of fear—it's inspiring others to move beyond it.
> —NELSON MANDELA, FORMER PRESIDENT OF SOUTH AFRICA

A friend once told me that life and leadership are a lot like baseball. Even the best batters strike out sometimes. But a true athlete can never run away from the plate. When time slows and the pitcher winds up and the whole world seems to hold its breath, he knows that he may hit the ball and he may not. But what is important is that he doesn't run from the plate; he displays courage in giving his best and taking the risk.

As a snow skier, that analogy is helpful to me. I remember

the first time I faced the challenge of a mogul run on a black-diamond slope. Steep and overwhelming. It was tough for me to muster the energy to get started down the mountain. While gazing over the side from the top of the run, my friend's advice was, "Point your skis down the hill and keep your nose over your tips. You have to lean forward and over your ski tips."

He reminded me to lean into the mountain:

> The key in steep mogul skiing is to focus on the moguls you are hitting next, not the moguls you are hitting now. Put your nose out over the tips of your skis, even though it feels like you will fall face-forward out of control. Even when you are overcome with fright, maintain a posture of nose over tips, rather than leaning back. Lean back and you fall.

This is not only great advice for skiing steep slopes but also good advice for leadership. As a leader, you sit atop the mountain. You have no choice but to face the slopes. You have a choice either to lean back, coast, and play it safe, or you can snowplow your way back and forth across the mountain and dominate the run. Being a courageous leader requires you to push beyond the norm and be willing to take risks.

Writer Jamie Walters penned an article for *Inc*. magazine that lays out the importance of courage in the workplace. He notes that small acts of courage are possible every day, but we shy away from such deeds due to our fears of "rocking the status quo." We choose not to speak up or share alternative viewpoints. We choose not to advocate for a possible new hire who shows potential but lacks experience. We choose not to provide honest counsel that may hurt another's feelings. We choose to settle for the familiar rather than to embrace the unknown. But these decisions are often detrimental, preventing us from transcending the roller-coaster ride we call business and creating a better workplace. Walters says:

> Imagine a group, department or company where "citizen-leaders" are invigorated by the notion that they can be courageous every week—regardless of their title or role. Picture the results of a team with such high morale and unified commitment to their own group mission, as well as the company's, that its members feel a true sense of ownership and responsibility. Or, visualize the leader who inspires a level of momentum that ushers in a new, more effective way of working and a stronger sense of purpose. All are possible, and each requires courage.[2]

This essential element is one of the common elements of biblical leaders. Abraham left his home to journey to a place he wasn't even sure existed. Moses overcame his speech impediment to lead the people of Israel to freedom. Joshua faced doubters who feared the promised land was too difficult to conquer. "Be strong and courageous," Joshua said (Joshua 1:9).

SHARE ON 🐦 📘
Don't play it safe. Chase after something so much bigger than you are, there's no way you could ever accomplish it without God. #CatalystLeader

Gideon led an army of only three hundred to defeat an army of thousands. Daniel and Esther displayed tremendous courage in the face of death. Nehemiah overcame fierce opposition to rebuild the walls of Jerusalem in fifty-two days. Jesus faced the cross and triumphed over death. Paul penned parts of the New Testament while nurturing wounds in prison; and nearly every apostle preached the gospel until being martyred.

I love Jesus' words in John 16:33: "I have told you these things, so that in me you may have peace. In this world you will have trouble. But take heart! I have overcome the world" (NIV). The Christian life is one that holds in tension both realism and idealism. It accepts life's uncertainties and inevitabilities but recognizes that hope remains. Following Jesus does not mean we will not falter or fail or fear, but rather that in the midst of those realities we are able to "take heart."

The record of Christian history illustrates this legacy of taking heart amid life's difficulties. Martin Luther nailed his ninety-five theses to the Wittenberg church door and catalyzed the Protestant Reformation. William Wilberforce dreamed of a society free of slavery, and he began a movement to realize it. Hudson Taylor braved the seas and became the first missionary in China. In 1930 George Washington Carver turned down every job opportunity and instead chose to courageously enhance the lives of poor Southern farmers. Dietrich Bonhoeffer stood against the Nazi regime and ultimately gave his life opposing the evil dictatorship. In

1955 Rosa Parks literally took a courageous seat of liberation, changing the course of human history. And in 1963 Martin Luther King Jr. had a dream, and today we still feel the impact of his courageous march toward freedom.

The lives of great Christian leaders teach us that those who follow a God-sized calling need God-sized courage. They embody the psalmist's words: "Be strong and let your heart take courage, all you who hope in the LORD" (Psalm 31:24). Do you hope in the Lord? Then be courageous, the psalmist says.

> We ought to be radical revolutionaries taking great risks to advance the cause of Christ. The purpose of life is not to arrive at death safely. . . . God is looking for a generation that would dare to trust him to do incredible things in and through their lives.
>
> —CHRISTINE CAINE, COFOUNDER OF THE A21 CAMPAIGN

Today, the influencers I respect most are the ones who live and lead bravely. I think of people like Manny Martinez, cofounder of Hello Somebody. After encountering hungry children in a developing country, his heart was enlivened. He noticed that there was great need all around him that was going unnoticed and unaddressed. A phrase began ringing in his ears: "Hello somebody. Is anyone listening?"

Not knowing how he could accomplish his goal, he and some friends set out to provide a million meals in one calendar year. Today, Hello Somebody works to provide food, hydration, education, and freedom to children. And they've become a major player in the fight against sex trafficking.

Hannah Song, president of LiNK (Liberty in North Korea), works in one of the most dangerous countries on earth. They rescue refugees who have escaped and resettle them in South Korean and American shelters. They've raised global awareness about the human rights crisis in North Korea and are leading the effort to provide emergency relief to refugees. For her, the risk of danger is not as great as the promise of freedom.

Consider pastor Muriithi Wanjau, a church planter in the heart of Nairobi, Kenya. He is turning ordinary people into fearless influencers of society. He has embarked on a courageous strategy to raise up Christ-followers in the middle class to fight poverty across the African continent.

**Keys for a Courageous Lifestyle
from Christine Caine (video clip)
http://catalystleader.com/christinecainecourage**

Here in the United States, I think of Aaron Smith, who started Venture Expeditions as a college student more than a decade ago. Instead of accepting the security of a regular job, he chose to launch this nonprofit, which helps leaders discover their passions through adventure-driven humanitarian efforts that raise money for worthy Christian organizations. Aaron began by biking across America, more than three thousand miles from the West Coast to the East. The expedition raised more than seventeen thousand dollars for a South American congregation. Today, Venture Expeditions leads multiple teams on courageous journeys for charitable causes and has raised hundreds of thousands of dollars for partner organizations.

I also think of Scotty Smiley, a guest of ours at Catalyst Dallas in 2011, who is a modern hero who was severely injured in the line of fire in Iraq, losing his eyesight. Since then, in 2007, he has climbed mountains, snow-skied, surfed, and participated in many other activities. He is the first blind officer in the US Army and continues to serve his country at the US Military Academy at West Point as an instructor. His quote from our interview together still stands out in my mind:

> No matter what's placed in front of us, we should live life like it's the last day. As opportunities arise for me and are given to me, I take those opportunities and grab them and do everything I can. Courage is not only just doing things when it's easy, but it's doing things, and the right things, when it's hard. Choosing the harder right versus the easier wrong.

I admire Jarrett and Jeannie Stevens, who planted a church in urban Chicago. Jeannie talks about how much faith it required to step out and start a new congregation. She says it was one of the hardest faith adventures of her life and required another commitment to be disrupted. She says she heard God encourage her: *I've called you to courage. Do you trust Me?* Jarrett and Jeannie answered yes, as every change maker must.

What each of these leaders knows is the same thing the greatest leaders in Scripture and Christian history knew: courage is an essential element of leading well. Their hope overtakes their fear. It calls them to confront and to push forward, even when everything inside beckons them to shrink back. And in the process, their courage places them in the context of a larger story of what God is accomplishing in our midst.

A Lifetime of Leading Well: John Perkins

A sharecropper's son who grew up a poor child in Mississippi, John Perkins fled to California at seventeen years old, after a town marshal murdered his older brother. After devoting his life to Christ in 1960, he returned to his home state with a message of forgiveness through the power of the gospel and justice through racial equality. His efforts were repaid with imprisonment, beatings, and all kinds of harassment. But he didn't give up.

Perkins is a hero, and after spending time around him and seeing his true humility and authenticity, I give him even greater respect. This giant of a man has stared down and faced some of the greatest challenges of the last hundred years. He defines *courage* as living one's conviction in the face of fear. He reminds us that fear can be a speed bump, but it should never be a stop sign. Standing directly in front of what causes us fear brings our convictions to the forefront.

Dr. Perkins speaks to students and young leaders all over the country. And he is full of hope and vision for the future, evidenced by his comments from our Catalyst Dallas event in 2011:

I think this generation, they more or less want to be defined by their love for Jesus Christ and, importantly, they are doing something. . . . Many are doubting that this generation can deliver us. I've got faith in this generation. We know that these problems are beyond our social-economic problems, these have a spiritual dimension that's got to be tied together with the social-economic and we've got to inspire people so they can both own the problem and get the joy of working with the solution.

Perkins's life has been built on overcoming barriers and obstacles in Jesus' name, so the decision to offer him the Catalyst Lifetime Achievement Award wasn't a difficult one. He's helped restore dignity and pride to African-Americans in his community, and has literally risked his life to live out his calling. More than eighty years old now, Perkins moves a little slower than he once did, but he still has the courageous heart of the young man who risked his life to stand in the face of evil.

ORGANIZATIONAL COURAGE

Courage is not just an individual trait but an organizational one. The leaders at Saddleback Church know this. When pastor Rick Warren was asked in a Catalyst podcast interview about what makes a healthy church, he mentioned courage as indispensable. He pointed out that every major advance at Saddleback required a risk in every major decision that scared him to death, but he did it anyway. As a result of their belief that

God must be trusted and leaders must be brave, Saddleback's leadership has named "risky faith" as one of their core values.

Do the thing you fear the most," Rick advised. "Leading with authentic honesty is required as well in taking risks. I have a church that would march into hell with squirt guns because we've modeled faith and taking risks.

One common denominator in every church that God has His hand on is the faith factor. Leadership that is not afraid or fearful to believe God and take risks. Faithfulness is taking risks. If I'm not taking any risks, I don't need any faith. Walk directly toward the things you fear the most. If I don't need any faith, then I'm being unfaithful.[3]

We've tried to model this characteristic at Catalyst. Our team made a decision to add our West Coast and One Day events in the same year. We went from one event to six in a short span without adding any staff. Our team wasn't sure how we'd pull it off and worried that we might cannibalize our flagship gathering in Atlanta, but we decided to move forward nonetheless.

Our team recognized the success of our Atlanta event but sensed that we had more to accomplish. In making this decision, we risked failure. But had we chosen not to move forward, we felt we'd risk even more. To our surprise, our courage was rewarded. The One Day events filled up with more than six thousand attendees; we had thirty-five hundred attendees at our West Coast event; and the Atlanta gathering still filled up.

We desire for the Catalyst community to adopt a spirit of courage in work too. So in 2011, we chose "Take Courage" as the theme for our Catalyst West and Catalyst Dallas events. We desired to push people out of their comfort zones in order to provoke them to grow. So we placed a single question in front of our participants: "What if you stepped into all God has created you to be?"

We know that all leaders confront fear of failure and fear of the unknown. But living in that fear is destructive for a team and will kill momentum. We know that the road is long and the pressures are great. And in the face of these strains, we want our community to take courage.

At this event, Andy Stanley spoke about courage, which he believes is the most important trait a leader can possess. "Many, many great things have begun with a single act of courage. Throughout history and today. A person steps out and makes one courageous decision and that one domino starts many other dominoes falling," Stanley said. "We have to step out and take that first step, and we may never know the ripple effect of that one courageous decision. Catalyst leaders—your decision to do something courageous may result in something greater than you ever imagined. Step out."[4]

Courage is not waiting for your fear to go away. We know this at the gut level, but many times fear is still what holds us back. Andy goes on to say, "Fear in leadership usually is connected to the uncertainty about the future. But uncertainty about the future is never going to go away. I tell leaders all the time—uncertainty is why there are leaders. Uncertainty gives you job security. Wherever there is uncertainty, there will always be a need for leaders, which means always stepping out into the unknown, always requiring courage."

Author and speaker Nancy Ortberg took the idea of courageous leadership a step further, urging leaders to inject the personal trait into their organizational DNA. At our gathering in Los Angeles in 2011, she shared her conviction that creating a courageous culture is critical to succeeding:

SHARE ON 🐦 📘
What would you pursue today if you weren't afraid to fail? If you knew for certain that you were the one to make it happen? Go do that.
#CatalystLeader

"Courage is not gender specific, and it doesn't require an education, an age limit, or a résumé. Every single one of us is capable of transferring courage from God into our organization. Courage is the kind of virtue that without it none of the other virtues of leadership is possible. The only way to courage is through fear and obstacles, frustration and surrender."

Recently, I had to let a longtime team member go. He was no longer a good fit for our organization as we moved into a new phase. We needed to make a change, but I was hesitant to have a tough conversation. I wanted to honor his time with Catalyst and the contributions he'd made over the years. But I also wanted to release him to pursue something he'd be better suited for. I struggled with having an already tough conversation because he was a friend and because he didn't recognize that this needed to happen. I waited too long to tell him, putting it at the bottom of my to-do list every day and trying to ignore it, which made it worse. When I finally did, he confronted me for sitting on it. His frustration was justified. I had let my own fears, insecurities, and emotions get in the way of executing courageously. Always confront the tough decisions or conversations head-on.

**Watch Nancy Ortberg's Talk on Courage
from Catalyst West, 2011 (video clip)
http://catalystleader.com/nancyortbergcourage**

Here are some helpful tips for building a culture of courage in your organization:

- *Set scary standards.* Your level of excellence and expectation for your product or service or experience should almost be something that is nearly unattainable. Safe goals are set by safe leaders with safe visions. Give your people a goal that scares them, and you'll produce leaders who know what it means to overcome fear.
- *Allow for failure.* The road to success is many times put together through multiple failures. Allow for and even encourage your team to fail as they attempt to succeed.
- *Reward innovation.* Innovation requires taking risks.

And bold risks create bold team members. Rewarding innovation will challenge your team to grow in their roles.

- *Pursue the right opportunities.* Not every risk is a good one. Be disciplined. Aggressively pursue a few things that make sense. Say no often.

- *Learn to delegate.* This is one of the most courageous things a leader can do. Entrusting others with important tasks requires letting go and relinquishing control. Liberally pass responsibility and authority to your team. If you want your team to be courageous, give them the chance to lead.

These elements aren't easy to nurture in a corporate or ministry setting. According to our research, a mere 2 percent of Christian leaders believe "courage" is the trait that best describes them. You will likely resist it at every turn. As G. K. Chesterton said, "Courage is almost a contradiction in terms. It means a strong desire to live, taking the form of readiness to die."[5] Courage mingles our desire to rush forward with a willingness to accept the possibility of being stopped in our tracks.

How to Be a "Face in the Mud" Leader
http://catalystleader.com/faceinthemud

Yet those who desire to be change makers have no choice; they must exhibit courage. Any leader who achieves something significant has, at one time, arrived at a moment of great uncertainty.

- Should we launch a building campaign or add another church service?
- Should we hire new employees?
- Should we start our own business?
- Should we invest in this promising but unproven technology?

Moving forward requires a great risk, but the possibility of running away somehow feels more perilous. In those moments, the change maker will need a deep trust in God's sovereignty and a heavy dose of bravery to lunge forward. One's natural leadership abilities are sufficient to survey the options. But action requires an unusual dose of courage.

Courage is not inborn like some other leadership essentials. It's learned. The natural human response is to run away from what frightens us. But life's greatest leaps occur when we resist this impulse. Remember when you were completely fearless as a kid? Children often demonstrate courage naturally. Most of us can think back to times as a child when we stepped out in courage. Whether

SHARE ON 🐦 📘
The road to success is many times put together through multiple failures. Allow for and even encourage your team to fail as they attempt to succeed. #CatalystLeader

riding a bike without training wheels, jumping into the deep end of the pool, or letting go of the rails to ice-skate without assistance, we learned that progress requires courage. We have to be willing to get out to the edge, look at what is in front of us, summon up the fortitude, and jump.

I can remember as a child walking out on the end of the high dive at the Bristow City Pool, scared to death. The first time I jumped off the high dive, I thought for sure my head would explode. Once I hit the water, and actually survived, I felt the confidence to quickly move on to trying a flip, and then ultimately the Olympic team! It is a lesson that is seared in my mind: attacking my fear head-on allowed me to accomplish something I never thought possible. The same with mountain climbing in Colorado. I'm definitely no expert, but the key to mountain climbing is fearless pursuit to the top. Put one foot in front of the other and continue to make gradual progress on your way up the mountain.

Making a difference many times starts with just simply making a move. We can't live and lead in a state of fear and inactivity. Don't sit on the sidelines. As believers, as followers of Jesus, if we're not chasing after something that is much bigger than we are—and there's no way we could ever accomplish it without God—then we are playing it too safe.

The film *Braveheart* offers one of the greatest examples of courage in modern cinema. It's one of my top-five favorite movies. I've seen it more than twenty times, and it still inspires me and pushes me to my feet cheering. I, too, want to charge the castle and fight for the principles I hold dear.

Randall Wallace wrote the screenplay and produced the movie, and he has spoken at multiple Catalyst events. A legendary figure in Hollywood, he's also produced films such as *Secretariat* and *We Were Soldiers*. A common theme in each of these storylines is courage in the face of adversity. The trait makes for a great movie, but it also is an essential for being a catalyst leader. We must remember, as the character William Wallace so aptly reminds, "Men don't follow titles. They follow courage."

Jim Daly has realized this truth. As the president of Focus on the Family, his approach has been to try to build bridges with many organizations and leaders, even those who deeply disagree with Focus. Following the tenure of the iconic James Dobson, he had to make significant changes. This has cost him, but Focus has benefited. Daly embodies much of what living courageously is about. He's changed the entire face of the organization, and his work has been hailed as refreshing and inspiring.

SHARE ON
Courage calls us to confront and push, even when everything inside of us beckons us away from it.
#CatalystLeader

Today's leaders want to be part of organizations built on this level of bravery. They want to follow leaders up the hill. They want to join a team that beats the odds and perseveres through doubt. They want to jump. But we must be intentional about developing this unnatural characteristic. I often write down a list of ten things I'm afraid of and then let a friend pick three I'll attempt to conquer this week. I think back on the last six months and ask, "Is there something God's nudged me on that I've ignored?" These are good exercises for any leader who wants to lead boldly, and they will empower you to lead well.

What if we stepped into all God has created us to be? "Fear not" and "do not be afraid," Scripture reminds us. No matter what your calling or what challenges you're confronting, every leader must make a choice. You can sit on the mountaintop and enjoy the view, or you can leap into the free fall of riskiness. You can appreciate all you've accomplished, or you can step off the ledge and take the plunge. Take it from me. The jump may be risky, but the decision to stay where you are is even more so.

FIVE COURAGEOUS LEADERS YOU SHOULD KNOW

- HANNAH SONG | LINK GLOBAL

   North Korea is not a country for the fearful. The oppressive government has robbed its people of their freedoms and will punish any who challenge their authority. Yet Hannah has begun a project that rescues refugees and resettles them in LiNK Global shelters in China. For her, the risk of danger is not as great as the promise of freedom.

- SHANNON SEDGWICK DAVIS | BRIDGEWAY FOUNDATION

   An attorney by trade, you won't find Shannon litigating divorce cases today. Instead she's devoted her life to fighting genocide and promoting human rights around the globe. Through Bridgeway Foundation, she raises money to fund her efforts to track down the world's most notorious perpetrators of genocide, trafficking, and other crimes against humanity, and bring them to justice.

- JONATHAN OLINGER | DISCOVER THE JOURNEY

   Discover the Journey is a team of brave journalists and storytellers who work to expose injustices against children through the production of media and art. Leading the organization is Jonathan Olinger, who has traveled to some of the world's most dangerous and destitute places—Haiti, DR Congo, Iraq, and

Zimbabwe—in search of crises that need greater attention.

- ## CUE JEAN-MARIE | NEWSONG LA COVENANT CHURCH

  If courage is measured by caring for "the least of these" at all costs, then Cue might be one of the most courageous people I know. He grew up a poor, drug-addicted gang member, but things changed once he met Jesus. Today, he works in the infamous Central City East area of LA—known by many as skid row. The area contains one of America's largest homeless populations and is riddled with crime, but Cue has devoted his life to bringing hope and peace to its residents.

- ## ANTHONY ROBLES | WRESTLING CHAMPION AND COACH

  Becoming a wrestler takes courage, but becoming a wrestler when you were born with only one leg requires a mountain of it. Anthony recognized his passion for wrestling in eighth grade and bucked the naysayers to train and master the sport. He finished high school with a record of 129–15 and won the 2010–2011 NCAA wrestling championship for his weight class. If only more dreamers would pursue their passions with such unbridled bravery.

6

PRINCIPLED

ANCHOR IN YOUR CONVICTIONS

Greatness is not about personality. It's about humility, plus
will. That is where the essence of leadership begins.

—JIM COLLINS, CATALYST ATLANTA

EVERY ORGANIZATION'S COMMITMENT TO INTEGRITY WILL BE
tested sooner or later. Our team faced our test the year before
I took over as president of Catalyst. And we failed.

We had been planning the event for months under the
pressure of a strained budget. Our team desired to produce a
quality event, but we also wanted to survive. In a moment of
frustration, a large Christian organization swooped in with
a lucrative offer. They offered to write a check to become a
top-level sponsor in exchange for the right to help shape our

program. This included selecting some of our main stage speakers.

I wish I could say that our leadership debated the choice for days or even weeks, that they closed themselves in an office and fervently prayed over the decision. But I can't. With the need for a cash infusion, we accepted the offer and began planning our event accordingly.

When the event finally arrived, our team hoped for the best. But the best always seemed to evade us. Several of the sponsor-selected speakers bombed. They weren't prepared for the opportunity, but rather had been chosen to boost the sponsor's brand in the minds of our community. Carefully crafted advertisements for our supporter and their products were crammed between presentations. The event began to feel like difficult-to-watch infomercials sewn together with an awkward thread.

To their credit, the audience reacted with a lot of frustration and a little bit of fury. We received negative letters and e-mails by the boatload following the event. People complained about the forced programming and thin presentations. They assured us they would not be returning if this is what Catalyst planned to become.

We reeled for months after our poor showing. Disappointment morphed into discouragement. Morale sank. We all knew we had compromised our integrity. Our team had failed, and because I didn't speak up, I had failed too.

As our team evaluated the event and discussed our

future, a common desire to renew our commitment to integrity rose up. Though we had failed, we didn't have to become failures. Together we decided to right our wrong and to ensure the blunder would never be duplicated. We defined the core values of our organization and made a pact to keep each other accountable to uphold them at all costs. And then we selected our theme for the next year: "Vintage." We set out to assure our community that we were returning to who we once were—to the organization and leadership community we wanted to be.

Catalyst learned many valuable lessons through this ordeal. We learned that every organization fails, and we were no exception. We learned that failures can become successes if you learn from them. We learned who we were and who we wanted to be, and outlined a system to prevent a recurrence of our mistakes. Our greatest error became one of our greatest advancements.

I carried this lesson with me into my new role leading Catalyst. I determined to be uncompromising in our commitment to our principles. Today, you cannot purchase a speaking slot at any of our events. The Catalyst stage is not for sale. Leading with character is the standard for every decision we make and the foundation for how we interact with one another and with our community of leaders. We will not compromise this.

In some ways I picked this up from my father. When he said something, you could believe it. He was unfailingly honest. If he got extra change, he wouldn't pocket it. Dad never broke a promise to me, he made his family a priority, and he always treated people with respect and kindness. I grew up watching my father lead by his principles and protect his reputation, and he taught us to do the same. Like him, I recognize that an individual or an organization must define their character and stick to it.

The homespun phrases my father would use to prod me during childhood included:

- *If it is worth doing, it's worth doing right.*
- *It's not what you say; it's what you do.*
- *Don't start what you won't finish.*
- *Whether you win or lose, you'll learn.*
- *Your word is your bond. If you can't keep it, don't give it.*

I can still remember hauling hay on a one-hundred-degree Oklahoma summer day or building a fence one early Saturday morning in the fall following a late-night high school football game, and having him drop one of these gems on me in mid-conversation. Over time, they seared my mind and stuck in my gut.

I recall how frustrated I felt when my dad reminded me how important it was to stack hay bales in perfect alignment. It didn't matter to me at the time. No one would ever inspect our work, measure it for effectiveness, or worry about how straight the bales were. But to my dad, it was about discipline and living out the lessons he was trying to teach me. The important piece was that *we* would know the quality of our work and how well it was done, regardless of whether anyone else did.

Steve Jobs, cofounder of Apple, was similarly shaped by his father during childhood. Steve talked about the importance his father placed on crafting the backs of cabinets and fences properly, even though they were hidden. "He loved doing things right. He even cared about the look of the parts you couldn't see," Jobs later remarked.[1] Like Steve, my dad valued work that reflected the best in me and was rooted in something deeper than duty.

These lessons came in handy when our organization faced periods of turmoil and distraction, when we were tempted to compromise who we are and what we believe. There was a period of years when Catalyst's parent company was bought and sold. Our future was uncertain as well as our ability to maintain what we created. Catalyst has had many people in high levels of leadership with ideas about what Catalyst should be or should've been or how it could be better. Those ideas often compete with one another. We faced organizational distractions and the temptation to change course more than a handful of times. Without a commitment to our core values, we would be a ship at sea during a tempest.

Catalyst
Core Values

- A high standard of excellence
- Work hard, play hard
- A culture of family
- Passion for Jesus
- Approachable, real, and comfortable with who we are
- A heart for leaders

I've learned that leaders are defined by their inner strengths and convictions, not the outer portrayal of who they are. Your character will determine your level of leadership and even your legacy. Reputation can't be delegated, and as we well know, it takes a lifetime to build but only a few seconds to lose. Living on principle is one essential that will help you not only lead well but also finish well.

THREE ELEMENTS OF PRINCIPLED LEADERSHIP

A principled life is composed of at least three essential elements. Though these are not the only elements, they rank among the most important. Without committing to these three elements, leading is nearly impossible. The first is humility.

Element #1: Humility

The influencers among the next generation who are leading well are also the humblest people I know. They don't need the credit for the impact of their books, organizations, or churches. They lead without gobbling up the spotlight. When I compliment them, they often turn the conversation back to their staff and God's grace. I call this "ego leak," or the practice of ridding oneself of pride through the pipeline of praising others. It's a sure mark of a humble leader. The best leaders are reflectors of praise, not absorbers.

SHARE ON 🐦 📘
A catalyst leader is humble and hungry, not arrogant and entitled.
#CatalystLeader

Humble leaders are also honest about their flaws and failures. They don't cover them up; they embrace them. "Humility is not denying your strengths," says Rick Warren. "Humility is being honest about your weaknesses."[2] When leaders are confident in their abilities and trust God for the outcome, they are comfortable with the chinks in their armor. But when they brag on themselves and sweep their foibles under the rug, you can bet that they are wrestling with their own pride and insecurities. Humble leaders are willing to pass on the credit but absorb the criticism, push others higher while making themselves lower, and put the desires of the team ahead of their own.

I've learned that the way a person speaks often reveals

much about his or her level of humility. To test whether you're leading humbly, search your speech for these phrases:

- *"I'm sorry."* Humble leaders are quick to apologize when they misstep. If you can't say these two words, resentment will spread throughout your team. Apologizing for your mistakes will turn resentment into respect.
- *"That was my fault."* Leaders are often afraid to admit mistakes to their team. But you can guarantee that the team already knows who is responsible for a failure. You will gain more respect by owning your mistakes than by ignoring them.
- *"Thank you."* Expressing gratitude is one of the greatest tools for boosting morale. Think of small ways to express thanks. A team that feels appreciated will work harder for you and remain loyal to you when times get tough.
- *"I'm listening."* President Calvin Coolidge once said, "No man ever listened himself out of a job." Stop talking once in a while and simply listen to what your team is saying. You'll learn much about your organization and yourself if you'll close your lips for an hour or two. When I'm in a meeting, I try to ask twice as many questions as I give answers. Often I learn things I would never have known otherwise.

- *"I trust you."* One of the least communicated phrases is also one of the most important. Your team needs to know you have confidence in them and in their ability to execute their jobs. Slay the micromanager who sits on your shoulder and affirm your trust for those who work alongside you.
- *"Great job."* Encouragement is one of the most powerful components in a leader's arsenal. My friend Steve Graves calls this handing out "ego biscuits." Be generous and liberal with encouragement.

Humility can't be taught, but at Catalyst we attempt to create internal conditions conducive to developing a contrite spirit. Our goal is that no one, including me, thinks too highly of himself or herself. When it comes to authority and responsibility, we've tried to push decision-making down as far as possible. We put little emphasis on hierarchical reporting structure; rather, we stress areas of focus and key initiatives.

At Catalyst, any of our team members can approach me with a problem or issue or idea. We believe this structure keeps job titles from inflating egos. We don't take ourselves too seriously, and that starts with me. We value an approachable culture free of power-tripping kings and queens. No one on our team considers himself too important to jump in and pack boxes or carry bookshelves or do what seem to be mundane tasks.

Seven Signs You're "Too Big for Your Britches"

1. You feel like you need an entourage everywhere you go.
2. You're unreachable, using systems and handlers to shield you from others.
3. The only people you make time for are those who can do something for you.
4. You speak and offer advice *far* more than you ask questions and take notes.
5. You quit laughing, especially at yourself.
6. You feel certain jobs are beneath you and would be offended if someone asked you to perform those tasks.
7. You feel no one's work ever meets your approval—except your own.

Humble leaders don't need praise, accolades, or credit in order to perform. They listen more than they talk. They may be lesser known but are often more influential. They lead without stopping for fanfare or pats on the back. We've all been around prideful leaders who constantly talk about themselves and tell everyone how great they are. By contrast, humble leaders know that life does not orbit around their nameplate. They don't view themselves as too important to perform a task "below their pay grade." If needed, they may be seen taking out the trash, carrying boxes to the warehouse, or washing the dishes that have piled up in the break room. Hype never trumps hustle or humility.

Eugene Cho, founder of One Day's Wages, believes humans have the capacity to eliminate extreme poverty. His organization challenges leaders to give up a single day's earnings to help make this vision become a reality. Eugene says that pride is the greatest hindrance to leaders today. The remedy? He says, "Fight it, confess it, name it, and share it with others. But pursue humility without announcing it so that we don't become righteous about that and thus, have a more nuanced and sophisticated version of the same thing."[3] When our team senses pride, we try to stomp it out immediately.

A famous story is told of evangelist Billy Graham's sixtieth birthday party in Charlotte, North Carolina. The event was filled with well-known religious leaders, politicians, and dignitaries who each heaped praise on the world-renowned preacher. When Graham took the podium to offer his own remarks, he didn't express gratitude for all the compliments. Instead, he quoted Scripture: "God will not share His glory with another." He then asked them not to tempt him to steal God's glory by their praise, though he appreciated the kind words.[4]

Unfortunately, this level of humility is in increasingly short supply among leaders today. When we asked Christian leaders which leadership trait best described them, only 1 percent said "humility." Living in the First World provides us with a blessed existence, but it is often accompanied by a sense of entitlement. Yet more than one in four respondents to our survey said they look for humility in a potential boss. We need humble leaders who quietly accomplish great feats without dragging along the tumor of pride. These types of leaders do exist, and a few rise above the rest.

Jud Wilhite may be the most unknown influential senior pastor in America. His congregation, Central Christian Church in Las Vegas, is one of the largest in the country. Yet Jud leads and impacts the city of Las Vegas with a quiet confidence that attracts twenty thousand attendees every Sunday. Quite a feat for a church in the heart of Sin City.

Another great example is Nathan Nockels, one of the most influential music producers today. But he's probably best known for being the husband of vocalist and songwriter Christy Nockels. Yet Nathan is incredibly talented as a musician himself. He spends countless hours each week in a studio, mixing and creating captivating melodies. Composing songs performed by artists ranging from Passion and Chris Tomlin to Kristian Stanfill, Nathan's music impacts millions. Of her husband, Christy says, "Musically he is brilliant. He lives out this 'made in secret' idea. He would hide behind a curtain and play on the stage if he could! He has a heart for music, and I love that. He continues to inspire me by his choices and the way he desires to be faithful with what is in front of him."[5]

John Featherston, a top executive with Chick-fil-A, comes to mind as well. When we first met, I was blown away by how little he talked about himself and how focused he was on getting to know me. The next meeting, I actually made a bet that I would ask him more questions than he asked me. It was like a Wild West shootout. We squared off and riddled each other with questions until neither was left standing. I kid, but the principle and lesson I learned from John stuck with me: humble yourself enough to focus on others.

> I think leadership just comes down to walking in a humility that allows you to learn from others and hear from others, that isn't quick to judge, that allows you to give people the benefit of the doubt until they prove otherwise.
>
> —MATT CHANDLER, PASTOR OF VILLAGE CHURCH

The greater your position, the more at risk you are for compromising this principle. Power is one of the great corruptors of would-be leaders. It's intoxicating. In his classic leadership book *In the Name of Jesus*, Henri Nouwen writes that the reason power is such a strong corrupter is "it seems easier to be God rather than to love God, easier to control people than to love people, easier to own life than to love life." Remember that your character and integrity is built over time in the insignificant moments when you think no one is watching. Nurture a spirit of humility as you seek to lead and you'll get results you previously thought impossible.

I dropped the ball on this essential recently during a conversation between our team and one of Catalyst's longtime strategic partners. We were discussing our organization's recent growth, and I talked for several minutes about all of *my* contributions to the success. I looked around the room while I spoke and noticed deflated looks on my team members' faces. The energy had been sucked out of the room. I realized I'd been on a self-centered power trip in an attempt to make myself look good. I quickly shifted my vocabulary from "me" to "we," giving credit to those around me who deserved it.

Remind yourself often that you aren't the only member on your team. When you achieve a big win and someone asks you your secret of success, begin your answer with "we" or "us" or "our," not "me" or "I" or "my." And then say a prayer of gratitude for having a team you can count on. If your organization is solely built on you, it won't last. Team matters. The people closest to you and who know you the best should be the ones who respect you the most.

Jim Collins observes:

Greatness is not about personality; it's about humility. Humility plus will. That is where the essence of leadership begins. But humility of a very special type. It is humility defined, an absolutely burning ambition that is channeled outward into a cause or an enterprise or set of values in a company or mission that is bigger than yourself. Combined with the utterly stoic role to do whatever it takes for that ambition.[6]

When I encountered this quote in Collins's book *Good to Great*, it was the first time I realized the true power of humility. What I once saw as weakness is actually an essential part of what makes great leaders great. Ever since then, I've been reminding myself that humility is an indispensable trait for anyone who wants to become a change maker.

SHARE ON 🐦 📘
Humble leaders are willing to pass on the credit but absorb the criticism, push others higher while making themselves lower, and put the desires of the team ahead of their own. #CatalystLeader

Dave Balter, founder and chief executive of the social marketing company BzzAgent, says that leaders must have humility or be destroyed by hubris. By sharing the spotlight and recognizing the value of others, he says, we empower ourselves to lead well:

If you're an ego-fueled leader, find humility today, before it's too late. Disregard the fawning fanboys and king-like power you feel right now. Instead, choose to recognize your place in the universe is no more important than anyone else's. Know you can learn from every single interaction— no matter the person's credentials.

Walking humbly with God is important both to leadership and to serving God. In fact, it's one of the three things the prophet Micah says the Lord requires of those who follow Him (Micah 6:8). As we chase after God, we stop looking at ourselves and begin focusing in on Him, seeking where He is leading, what He wants for us, and how we can serve Him better. So humility is not just about thinking less of ourselves, but thinking of Jesus more and more. Louie Giglio sums it up by saying, "If Jesus rode in low on a donkey, then we should go ahead and get down off of our high horse."[7]

Element #2: Discipline

Discipline is the second essential element of a principled life. When I consider young leaders who are truly making a difference—the ones whose organizations and projects are innovative and effective—the one characteristic they all share is a commitment to hard work.

When Major League Baseball pitcher Nolan Ryan was young, he realized he had developed a habit of throwing the ball as hard as he could as long as he could. This approach wasn't working early in his career. He was throwing wild and walking batters and losing games. "If I didn't make an adjustment or change, then I was going to be one of those players who was very gifted, but didn't make a lot out of it," Ryan reflects. "I had to learn to lean on my mind, not just my body."[8]

So what did Ryan learn in the process?

"It is important to know that to get to the top and to be

successful at the top requires two different skill sets," says Ryan. "A lot of people get here with the God-given ability, the gift that they received. But to stay here and have a lengthy career takes a commitment to make sacrifices that most won't continually make. Talent may get you here, but it takes work, real work, to stay here, and it takes development of the mental side of your game to separate yourself on this level."[9]

The Hall of Fame pitcher learned that discipline and hard work were critical to success, and his new approach to pitching paid off big time. When Ryan retired at the age of forty-six, he had a stunning 324 career victories. He had also set records for most career strikeouts (5,714), most strikeouts in a season (383), and most no-hitters in a career (7).

As we lead, we must continually engage in the act of self-questioning. I suggest writing down critical questions once a year and then answering them honestly:

- When I look at the sum total of my efforts this year, do I believe I've done my best work?
- Have I finished everything I've started, or have I left a wake of piecemeal projects behind?
- Did I give in to the temptation to cut corners, and if so, how can I protect myself from taking those shortcuts in the future?

Our team has often set our sights on inviting a particular high-level speaker to a Catalyst event. We know these invitations are long shots for us, but we pursue them anyway. I remember one best-selling author we invited a few years back who was not a Christian and doesn't speak at many religious events. When we first reached out to him, he turned us down flat. But we didn't relent. We didn't badger him, but we continued to pursue him. We persisted for nearly three years before he accepted the offer. Now, he has spoken at several of our events. When most other organizations would have given up and gone a different direction, we remained steadfast.

We also spent nine years focusing on doing one thing really well: putting on a great leadership experience for our core audience. We know that discipline is hampered by distractions. So we've drilled down to a single goal and fixed our gaze on that. I encourage you to do the same.

Leaders lead from who they are on the inside. And that is why the God who made us is so eager to remake us on the inside.

—GARY HAUGEN, PRESIDENT AND CEO OF INTERNATIONAL JUSTICE MISSION

This generation in particular falls into the trap of romanticism when it comes to work. So many often think that a job is going to be filled with excitement and promotions and purpose. They are often surprised when they discover how much hard work is required to lead well. This requires a large measure of discipline. Contrary to some misconceptions, my team doesn't spend most of our time in a creative lab dreaming up fun events or rubbing shoulders with *New York Times* best-selling authors, megachurch pastors, and celebrity bloggers. Most of our time is spent in our offices working long days to execute well the tasks that would often seem meaningless to those outside.

Our tendency as human beings is to favor the quick over the slow, the cheap over the expensive, and the easy over the difficult. That's why we often seek the fastest shortcut to the biggest bang. We want a homerun in one swing. A touchdown in one Hail Mary pass. A simple decision that generates millions in revenue. When we think we're on the cusp of such a moment, our adrenaline dials up and we instinctively step in.

Be an "All In" Leader
http://catalystleader.com/youallin

Living a life of faithfulness runs counter to these tendencies. It recognizes that following God often requires that we choose the slow, difficult, and costly. It means favoring the slow-burn, everyday discipline to the firework flash of the moment. The making of a leader takes time, even though our social-media–soaked world gives us a different impression. There are very few overnight successes, and most leaders who take shortcuts don't finish well. Becoming a change maker requires a continual steadfastness undergirded by a commitment to healthy habits and traits. It requires choosing a longer road when we might be tempted to cut a few corners. Shoring up the foundation of our personal character brick by brick. Remaining committed in the nitty-gritty and the mundane. A catalyst leader understands that influence is as much about the journey as it is the destination. In anonymity and obscurity is where most leaders are truly developed and made. Where ordinary creates the extraordinary. God cares about who you are becoming way more than what you are doing or accomplishing.[10]

Singer and songwriter Christy Nockels says this about the discipline of gaining influence:

> Being made in the secret, in the places where no one knows and sees is crucial for the next wave of leaders. I want to have longevity and stay faithful. God has never allowed our career to spike up to a crazy level. I would much rather have a steady climb of cultivating faithfulness. Let's finish strong and be persistent, let's have longevity and stay faithful. Whether hidden or small or a big platform or not having a gold record or a platinum album. There is huge value in the richness of cultivating faithfulness where we are right now.[11]

I tell leaders all the time, especially those younger and equally ambitious, to become experts now, even before they need to be. Part of being a disciplined leader is being ready. When it's your turn to come off the bench, when it's your turn to give your opinion and offer advice, when it's your turn to lead the project, you can step in and make it happen. Act, lead, dream, create, and deliver based on the job or position you want next, not the job or position you have now. Step into that role before you ever have it. Demand perfection from yourself before anyone else ever demands it of you. Hit homeruns in the now, but have a vision and hunger for something bigger. See where you want to be, and lead like you're already there.

> Talent doesn't win. Hard work, determination, and character wins. If you root your talent and ability in those things, then you have a powerful combination.
>
> —ERWIN MCMANUS, PASTOR AND AUTHOR

Being a steadfast leader means doing what you say you are going to do. Your "yes" is yes, and your "no" is no. Credibility is achieved through discipline and capability. People want to follow leaders who are credible—who do what they say they will do. Your team wants to believe that your word can be trusted, that you are passionate about the work you are doing, that you know where you are headed, and that you have the necessary knowledge, perseverance, and skill to lead.

If you begin a project, finish it—no matter how long it takes or how much energy it requires. If you're not giving your best, ask a friend or coworker to hold you accountable. If you fail, put in the time necessary to extract lessons from that mistake. And of course, invest a large amount of time in your own spiritual development. Make constant progress.

Progress in the process creates possibilities. Move the needle each day. Never stop growing and getting better. Be curious, committed, and coachable—always a student.

Part of being disciplined means forcing yourself to do things you're tempted not to but know you should. The great temptation for Christians is to allow one's efforts *for* God in the workplace to replace one's journey *with* God in everyday life. You must be disciplined enough to carve out time for the One who gives us the talents and life necessary for the work we do. When we are spiritually disciplined, we are often more vocationally effective.

A Lifetime of Leading Well: Dallas Willard

Dallas Willard is more than an author; he's also a model of character. As a professor of philosophy at the University of Southern California in Los Angeles, he could have spent his life publishing in peer-reviewed academic journals and giving highbrow lectures. Instead, Dallas has devoted much of his adult life to exploring a life of principled follower-ship of Jesus. His books explore issues such as prayer, discipleship, and the spiritual disciplines.

Dallas Willard is not your typical philosophy professor. He's guided by something much deeper. Dallas is committed to living a life of Christ-centered humility, integrity, and discipline, and he's helped thousands of others join him in the endeavor.

"To run the race well, to be faithful over few things, is our part.

And as we look at the road ahead, we must deal with details," he writes in *Renovation of the Heart: Putting on the Character of Christ*. "That is, we must take the particular things that slow us down and the sins that entangle us, and put them aside in a sensible, methodical way."[12]

I spent a few minutes with Dallas Willard a couple of years ago at a Catalyst event. We enjoyed a rare time of conversation together. As he spoke, I remember sensing the presence of the Holy Spirit more than any other time in my life. It was a benchmark moment for me. His actions, carefully weighed words, and modest tone told me that he lived out the principles he promoted. As he asked questions about me and about Catalyst, I remember being struck by his humility and authenticity. He was there to receive our Lifetime Achievement Award, and at that moment, I knew we had picked the right person.

Part of being a disciplined leader is repetition. When my dad coached my high school football team, he would often end a play by yelling three words: "Run it again!" He knew that the only way to ensure that the team would get it right at game time was to repeat it often in practice. He recognized that a championship is not won on game day. It's won in the months and months of hard work, of practice, of two-a-days, of the gut-wrenching hard work that shapes a team. So he forced us to commit to hard work, discipline, and repetition so we'd be great even when no one was in the stands.

What is true in sports is also true in communication.

The best speakers, teachers, and preachers know that repetition is critical to driving home a point and making it stick. When parents attempt to instill a principle in children, they apply the same wisdom, repeating an axiom over and over again. When organizational leaders cast a vision, the words can't be spoken once and then forgotten. They must be revisited, reframed, and repeated until they sink into the organization's cultural fabric. This is often difficult for leaders to do because we grow bored or distracted with the messages we know all too well. But what is true for coaches, communicators, and parents is true for leaders as well. We must all learn to unleash the power of repetition. We must commit ourselves to the tasks we've been given and stick with over the long haul.

SHARE ON 🐦 📘
Demand perfection from yourself, before anyone else demands it from you. Become an expert now, even before you need to be.
#CatalystLeader

A dream doesn't become reality through magic; it takes sweat, determination and hard work.
—**COLIN POWELL, FORMER US SECRETARY OF STATE**

Malcolm Gladwell says leaders become experts when they stay on the journey for at least ten thousand hours.[13] Jim Collins echoes this with his concept of a twenty-mile march.[14] It's not the short sprint that shapes us but the perseverance in a particular task. Be faithful in the small things. Our character and who we are as leaders is mostly created by how we behave and grow when no one is watching.

While many Christians are familiar with Louie and Shelley Giglio's work leading Passion events, they may not know that the couple has been doing this work for seventeen years. And they've been ministering to college students for twenty-five years. They demonstrate that being persistent is crucial to leadership and one of the most important characteristics of those in leadership today.

"The attention spans of leaders are getting swept away by the deficit of attention in our culture. We have to have an attention span that is longer than twenty minutes, or twenty days, or even a year or two," Louie says. "Longevity, commitment, and discipline is what really matters."[15]

The Giglios have committed to sticking with what they've started, and they've grown deep roots. They've fought through the difficult times and enjoyed the successful ones. They abandoned illusions of overnight success long ago. As a result, they've built one of the greatest movements of young Christians in modern American history.

10 Ways to Increase Your Personal Discipline and Get Things Done
http://catalystleader.com/getthingsdone

Element #3: Integrity

A final essential element to principled leadership is the one our team learned the hard way years ago: integrity. It is the first of John Maxwell's famous "21 Irrefutable Laws of Leadership."[16] Best-selling author on leadership Warren Bennis calls integrity "the most important characteristic of a leader."[17] Jack Welch, former GE executive, said integrity was his organization's "No. 1 value" in his memoir. He said they never had a corporate meeting where integrity wasn't emphasized in his closing remarks.

Integrity has been defined as "a voluntary and consistent adherence to a set of human characteristics and principles including honesty, respect, loyalty, accountability and trust that are applied to all facets of business operations."[18] Yet if we accept this definition, we must admit that we've witnessed the downfall of this characteristic over the last thirty or more years in almost every area of culture. Corporate scandals like Enron have rocked the business world. Televangelists' affairs and priests' molestation charges have shattered respect for religious institutions. Scandals among politicians, athletes, and celebrities dominate headlines. As a result, our generation has grown increasingly cynical.

In a world of skeptics and pessimists, people are more attracted than ever to leaders of integrity. If you're known as a person of character, you'll attract better employees and keep them longer. You'll draw more loyal clients and more raving fans. Society longs for leaders of integrity.

We plant sod where God wants to plant seed. He's more interested in growing our character than having us look finished.

—BOB GOFF, AUTHOR AND FOUNDER OF RESTORE INTERNATIONAL

According to our survey, 64 percent of respondents said they believe integrity is one of the most important leadership traits of the next decade. I couldn't agree more. But perhaps more interesting is that 57 percent of Christian leaders said that integrity is one of the most important attributes they look for in a boss. If you work to develop this essential in your life, you will rise above the pack and become the kind of leader who will attract better talent to your team.

In order to build integrity, you must begin by identifying land mines. *What are the areas in which you are most vulnerable? What are your hidden weaknesses that could blow up in your face?* This could be pornography, coworkers whom you are secretly attracted to, or uncontrollable greed. Once you identify these areas, establish an accountability system. Make the right thing easy to do and the wrong thing difficult. And ensure someone else is providing oversight. Leaders can't afford to be insulated, and accountability is one of the best ways to guard against it.

Unfortunately, many of my peers continue to wrestle with this. My friend Jim recently left his pastorate because of a marital failure. He traveled all the time and resisted the many warnings of spending too much time with "friends" while on the road. He wasn't intentional in trying to be absent of integrity, but slowly began to slide down a steady slippery slope. Lack of accountability and some poor decisions caused him to blow up his marriage and wreck his life.

I, too, struggle with land mines in my life. Achievement is my idol, and I often catch myself deriving worth from my accomplishments. I also sometimes fall into a scarcity mind-set instead of an abundance mind-set, worrying through sleepless nights about whether people will actually attend our events. If I'm not careful, I'll begin making impulsive and damaging decisions out of my anxiety. As a result of my land mines, I have asked a few of my team members to speak honestly to me whenever they see me falling into these traps. I've even created a personal board of directors made up of friends who know me well and have the freedom to call me to account on anything and everything. None of us is too good, too spiritual, or too moral to make mistakes.

SHARE ON 🐦 📘
Who you are becoming is way more important than what you are doing.
#CatalystLeader

Several years ago at Catalyst Atlanta, we decided to have a film crew follow me around during the event to capture what was going on. Everywhere I went a cameraman was just behind. At first, I enjoyed the novelty of it and didn't think much of it. But then it got to me. I began to feel important, powerful, and untouchable. The allure of being a really big deal was overtaking me. I even asked a couple of my team members to grab a change of clothes for me since I was "so busy" and needed to be on camera. Fortunately, my friend Jeff, who has worked with me for many years, pulled me aside to give me a reality check. He told me I was stepping on the land mine of pride and needed to be careful. He was right, and I made an adjustment.

Once you identify your own land mines, you must set up systems of accountability. I've witnessed many leaders over the last decade who simply became disconnected. In order to lead well, you must avoid insulating and isolating. Stay connected with people whom you can trust and be honest with. People to whom you give permission to peer below the surface and who are not impressed by you. Integrity is essential; therefore, accountability is one of the great engines of leadership longevity. Who speaks truth into your life? Who can honestly tell you when you are wrong and keep you in touch with reality?

Don't become untouchable and start thinking you're a big deal. Remain yourself. Stay grounded and in touch. You can't necessarily control your reputation, but you can control your character. Avoid surrounding yourself with an entourage of handlers who tell you only what you want to hear and aren't willing to tell you the truth. For many leaders, the greatest threat to our influence right now is our tendency to read our own press clippings and continually put up a wall around us that protects us from any kind of honest feedback.

You can't do everything. The person or organization that tries to do everything will do nothing well. Focus on a few things and be great at those things. Know it. Breathe it. Love it. Live it. And do it well. Do it with excellence. Do it with integrity.

—EUGENE CHO, PASTOR AND FOUNDER OF ONE DAY'S WAGES

When people see you living a life of integrity and accountability, they'll trust you. Take time on a regular basis to ask yourself difficult questions about your personal character. What kind of person are you when no one is looking? Are you the same person when you're by yourself that you are around others? Do you exercise integrity in the small decisions as well as the significant ones? The answers to questions like these will help you evaluate if you're developing this essential trait in your life or not.

If you lead long enough, you will make poor decisions. You will compromise when you shouldn't or stand firm when you need to flex. But integrity must always be in the forefront of your mind. Remember, character is built over time and in the small moments. The seemingly insignificant decisions you make when you think no one is watching or paying attention will carve your character. So don't overlook everyday opportunities to build up your integrity. These incremental tests compose one's greater character.

Our team once invited a controversial speaker who created quite a stir among our community. E-mails poured in from outraged individuals asking us to reconsider the invitation. Soon we found ourselves in a bind. On the one hand, we wanted to honor our request to him. We had already released conference materials advertising his involvement, and perhaps some people decided to attend in part because of his participation. On the other hand, we did not want to bring this speaker into an environment he might find hostile or antagonistic to his message. Nor did we want to platform a speaker whom our community so deeply opposed that they might not even give him a fair hearing.

An earnest meeting turned into a dozen or more before we decided to have the speaker participate in the event via video rather than live. I was frustrated and disappointed by our decision. And embarrassed. After all, it was my decision to invite him in the first place, so I felt like a failure.

If you were to ask members of our team today if we made the right decision, some would say yes and others no. But what everyone would tell you is that our discussions centered on answering the question, What is the right thing to do in this situation? Maintaining integrity was our standard for decision-making. We recognized that being a principled organization meant using integrity as a standard for decision-making.

> Leadership functions on the basis of trust, and when the
> trust is gone, the leader soon will be.
>
> —JOHN MAXWELL, SPEAKER AND AUTHOR

BRINGING IT ALL TOGETHER

One person whom I believe brings together all three elements of principled leadership is Nancy Duarte. Nancy has built one of the most respected and influential design firms in Silicon Valley called Duarte Design. For twenty-two years she's been building her company and constructing an excellent corporate culture.

While the company is not a Christian organization, Duarte Design is led by Nancy and her husband with integrity, humility, and discipline, integrating biblical principles constantly into their organizational culture. Duarte Design assists the world's leading companies with constructing and building presentations. Her clients include Apple, Google, Al Gore, Cisco, Facebook, TED Fellows, and many more. These organizations work with Nancy because they trust her. They accept her organization's emphasis on Christian principles because they lead her to organizational integrity.

Nancy underscores the way that being a principled leader can set someone up for incredible success. And like Nancy, a catalyst leader is rooted in something more than raw ambition.

He is defined by the inner strengths and convictions, not the outer portrayal of influence. Catalyst leaders strive to maintain high levels of character, rigorous amounts of discipline, and humble spirits. As Andy Stanley says, "Your heart is the starting place for character, and it's what gets God's attention. Character is what turns your giftedness into influence, and unleashes God's power."[19]

When these elements come together, one's influence almost always expands. The depth of your character determines the reach of your influence.

FIVE PRINCIPLED LEADERS YOU SHOULD KNOW

- NANCY SLEETH | BLESSED EARTH

     When her husband, Matthew, was an emergency-room physician, Nancy lived a comfortable life. Then God called the couple to embark on a faith and environmental journey. Making the difficult decision to give up their luxury and comforts, they now work full-time to promote care of God's creation in churches, seminaries, and faith communities across America.

- RYAN MEEKS | EASTLAKE CHURCH

     Many pastors come across as calculating or guarded, but Ryan Meeks is a straight shooter. You never wonder what he thinks or believes, because he's honest and trustworthy. The EastLake Church staff are deeply committed to a few core principles that drive everything they do, including turning away many potential congregation members because they are not fully committed to living and leading out of the core values of EastLake. Talk about living by your principles!

- VICKY BEECHING | MUSICIAN AND WORSHIP LEADER

     Some worship leaders attempt to construct a perfect stage persona, but not Vicky. She was chemically imbalanced and burned out from her travel schedule, and she had the integrity to admit and solve the problem. Her talk on "ways to avoid what happened to me" is one of the most principled, practical leadership talks I've heard.

- **RYAN O'NEAL | SLEEPING AT LAST**

  In a world full of counterfeit musicians with prepackaged and ripped-off sounds, Ryan and his band, Sleeping at Last, haven't sold out. By sticking to their principles and refusing to go mainstream, they've ironically broken into the mainstream world. His music has been featured in television shows and films including *Private Practice* and *Twilight: Breaking Dawn*.

- **JASON LOCY | FIVESTONE DESIGN**

  Some design firms take any project as long as the client is willing to pay, but Jason and his team have adopted a different business model. They only work on projects they believe in. They could have made more money building a business that focuses on sheer volume, but instead they say no more than they say yes. If you're lucky enough to garner a yes from FiveStone, however, the resulting design work promises to be stunning.

7

HOPEFUL

BUILD TOWARD A BETTER TOMORROW

Vision is the most powerful weapon in the leader's arsenal.

—**BILL HYBELS, CATALYST ONE DAY**

IN THE MIDST OF A BUSY DAY, MY OFFICE PHONE RANG. I CON-sidered ignoring it altogether—distractions always come at the most inopportune times—but after the fourth or fifth ring, I grabbed it while continuing to answer the hundreds of e-mails in my inbox.

"Yes?" I answered impatiently.

It was Ben Rough, a friend who worked with organizing international trips for Compassion International. As mentioned earlier, Compassion is a child-advocacy group that utilizes a sponsorship program to rescue poor children around the world from spiritual, physical, social, and economic poverty. Since 1952, Compassion has been providing children with food, shelter, education, healthcare, and Christian discipleship. Today, they serve more than 1.2 million children in more than two dozen countries.

Compassion is a longtime partner of Catalyst, but more importantly, I believe they do some of the best advocacy work of any Christian organization I know of. So on that busy day, if anything was worth stepping away for, this call was it. I gave Ben my full attention as he explained the reason for his call.

Since I had been connected with Compassion for so long, they felt like it was time for me to witness their work up close. If I was willing, they wanted me to travel to Rwanda so I could see what they were doing there. The departure date was only a few months out, but the staff at Compassion believed the opportunity was worth the ask.

The phone line fell silent as I considered his request. I surveyed all the work on my desk and to-do list. Taking this trip would create a bigger backlog. I grew anxious at the thought of traveling to Africa, a place that I'd never been and that may be dangerous. But then a little spontaneity sparked inside, and I said yes before I could catch it.

For the next couple of months, I focused mostly on work, giving little thought to the commitment I'd made. Then the time arrived to make good on my commitment. *What will the work of this famous organization be like? Should I expect something like I've seen on those early-morning infomercials*? A host of questions tumbled through my mind as I boarded the plane.

What seemed like a lifetime passed before our plane finally approached Kigali, the capital city. Upon descent, I was struck by the absence of lights that one typically sees when flying into a city. Darkness filled the expanse in all directions, giving our destination a certain eeriness and giving me my first Dorothy moment: "Toto, we're not in Atlanta anymore."

The Compassion team went to baggage claim to pick up our bags. My weary eyes began to droop as each bag popped out like Pez. When all the bags had emerged, mine was the only one that didn't make it. *Just my luck*, I thought. *What a way to start a trip.*

The bus ride to the hotel only made matters worse. Imagine the worst driver you can think of, and then picture that person as the best driver on the highway. Cars lurched out of the darkness, horns were blaring, turns were taken at nausea-inducing speeds. I've never been happier to get out of a vehicle and into a hotel.

My night was restless, filled with anxiety about my missing luggage and the uncertain events of the next day. I arose early and stepped out to look at the street. For the first time, I realized I was on the other side of the world. The smell of the air and the sounds of the highway were nothing like my quiet suburban street. I heard conversations everywhere, but I understood none of them.

Since Rwanda's capital city has a population of almost one million, I expected it to look like, well, a city. I was surprised to notice a vast landscape of tin-roofed houses and plaster buildings dotting the green mountain slope. Unlike American cities, Kigali is not laid out on a grid. From the air, it looks more like a jigsaw puzzle.

Ducking back inside, I realized it was almost time to depart. I met with our team and we re-boarded the minibus with reluctance. At high speeds, we headed to the Kigali genocide memorial. Dust billowed up from beneath the tires and obscured our view on all sides. When we finally stopped, the particles settled and we filed out of the bus and into the building. The complex was constructed to honor the nearly one million Rwandans who were murdered in 1994. Approximately 250,000 are buried on the memorial grounds. I began to realize that this country was attempting to rebuild with bricks of hope and the mortar of forgiveness.

Next, we headed to a Compassion project site and school. The modest building was constructed of brick and mud. A volleyball court sat next to a playground and a basketball court that doubled as a soccer field. Children dressed in matching uniforms rushed to meet us when we arrived. Joy filled the air, lifted by their laughter. We laughed with the children and played games, kicked soccer balls, and told jokes.

I expected to come rushing in and be the children's hero. I imagined I'd be surrounded by kids who had nothing and the novelty of my presence would make their day. But the opposite was true. We visited multiple Compassion projects, listened to the Compassion Rwanda staff, and connected with hundreds of children and their families and heard many of their stories. Everywhere we went, they lifted my spirit, teaching me about joy and contentment. Turning to leave from the last visit on our final afternoon, I realized these kids and families had way more impact on me than I had on them. These children who had nothing were filled with joy and hope for the future.

On my flight home, I pondered my experiences in Rwanda and came to a startling realization. Compassion isn't just providing help, but hope. Hope is a powerful tool to help overcome poverty. True poverty is often the absence of hope. The Scriptures ring true: when we fail to dream, to envision the potential of tomorrow, people grow desperate. I saw it up close. A glimpse of hope can change the world and move someone from despair to an inspired vision. Hope in the future is the most powerful antidote to poverty.

> If your actions inspire others to dream more, learn more,
> do more and become more, you are a leader.
> —JOHN QUINCY ADAMS, SIXTH PRESIDENT OF THE UNITED STATES

Compassion's most valuable asset is not education or food, as important as those are, but the ability to hope and dream about achieving a better life. Everywhere Compassion was at work, joy filled the air when desperation should have.

This is the fuel that drives their work. And, as I've witnessed, this also compels the next generation of Christian leaders.

HOPE UNHINGED

As I read the New Testament, I'm stunned by all the passages that talk of God's kingdom. This is the idea that the world can be better if God's grace can be unleashed upon it. Jesus and those who followed Him most closely are painters, rendering a picture of this world and beckoning us to partner with God in constructing it. Christians who are attuned to God's calling on their lives are dialed in to this idea.

Scripture is replete with models of visionary leadership. I think of Moses, who served as God's mouthpiece for Israelite vision casting. Or Paul, who created great vision in the hope of eternity. Or perhaps the apostle Peter, who led a group of revolutionaries with visionary courage.

Catalyst leaders look through the windshield rather than stare in the rearview mirror. They focus on the future and seek to inspire others to help them build it. To do this, they must give their teams reason to believe that tomorrow can be better than today. As Newark, New Jersey, mayor Cory Booker says, leaders need "hope unhinged." That's why some of the most influential organizations and leaders today maintain a strong sense of vision, rooted in a better world.

As a nine-year-old, Austin Gutwein was confronted with the reality of orphaned children in Africa. Five years later, he decided to do something about it. He launched Hoops of Hope, a nonprofit that raises awareness and funds. The organization challenges kids all over the world to shoot free throws and raise money for African children, specifically in Zambia.

A simple act morphed into a movement with incredible vision. Austin is an amazing kid. He and his dad, Dan, joined us for three days at Catalyst in 2009. Their story inspired me. When I was fourteen, I was not concerned with anything happening outside of my own little world. I certainly wasn't devising ways to solve problems in developing nations. I was focused on getting the high score on Pitfall in Atari! But Austin has a vision for spreading hope to those who have little.

Esther Havens brings hope to thousands around the world by giving dignity to those in poverty through the power of a portrait. She is an award-winning photographer who shoots all over the world for organizations such as charity:water. I love what she has to say about the power of a photograph:

> A photo is powerful and can make change happen. Photos need to be a catalyst for change to happen. I'm always thinking about how that particular powerful story behind the photograph can bring hope and change by being heard and seen.[1]

Derreck Kayongo started Global Soap Project because he wanted to bring hope to his friends and family back in Kenya. A former refugee, he was a guest at our Catalyst Atlanta event in 2011, and his incredible vision is to fight disease in Africa by taking used soap and repurposing it to send back for basic sanitation. Over two million children around the world die annually because of sanitation issues, mainly because they don't wash their hands. He makes about ten thousand bars of soap every day based on the eight hundred million bars of soap thrown away in US hotels each year. Simple objects can truly change the world!

Jeff Shinabarger models hope through a number of initiatives. The motto for his organization, Plywood People, is, "We will be known by the problems we solve." And not only known by the ideas we have but also by turning those ideas into action, into life. Jeff says,

> That happens many times just by doing something. You can gain influence by doing something. Even when you fail, it separates you, because you are willing to step out and pursue a courageous vision. The pursuit of problem solving actually gives you influence. Making a difference starts with making a move.

Stepping out leads to hope and vision.

When it comes to hope, I look to people like Scott Todd, who leads 58: (based on Isaiah 58), who believes we can wipe out extreme poverty. I also look to Jena Lee Nardella, who heads up Blood:Water Mission, which helps provide clean water to those who need it. I think of Blake Canterbury, who started BeRemedy to help solve everyday issues with people in his community through the power of social media. His tagline is "See the need; be the remedy," and his organization provides practical help for those in need.

> The visionary must light a flame. Those who choose to follow its light must work to keep it burning.
> —SIMON SINEK, AUTHOR

Leaders are dealers of hope, and we must give it away constantly and without bias. If a leader wants to make a mark on this world, he or she must have a compelling vision for his or her work. It must be hopeful and inspiring. Just as every leader should have a personal calling statement, he or she also needs a personal legacy statement. John Maxwell says people will describe your life in one sentence—so what is the sentence you want people to use to describe you when you leave this world? If you are young, make sure to sketch it with a pencil that has a fresh eraser, because you will refine this numerous times over your life.

A few months ago, I spent some time with the staff of Holy Trinity Brompton (HTB), a church in the heart of London. While there, I was surprised by the hopefulness that pervades their culture. They recently gathered over four thousand leaders in the Royal Albert Hall to proclaim the name of Jesus at the HTB Leadership Conference. This is a mammoth crowd, considering the state of religion in the United Kingdom. The spirit that drives them originates, in part, from their leader and vicar, Nicky Gumbel. Though he is a person of tremendous influence and power, he humbly rides his bike to and from the venues. He doesn't tote an entourage with him. He is incredibly humble, authentic, and inspiring. And he casts vision for the city of London and the world to his church and staff every chance he gets.

A Lifetime of Leading Well: Bill Hybels

Bill Hybels is a pastor's pastor. Known for his impeccable communication skills and legendary leadership, he's grown Willow Creek Community Church into one of the most influential congregations in America. Approximately twenty-four thousand people attend weekend services at his Chicago-area church, and more than nine thousand congregations in forty-five countries participate in his Willow Creek Association. Perhaps most interesting is Global Leadership Summit, an annual influencer gathering that Bill hosts. Nearly one hundred thousand leaders join this event at more than one hundred host sites.

What drives a person like Bill Hybels forward? What fuels his engine? In a word, *vision*. I've learned much from Bill over the years, primarily from his sermons and speeches on leadership and influence. He may be the best vision-caster I've ever known. In twenty minutes, Bill can paint a picture of a better future and stir hope in listeners' hearts that this future is possible. Every time I'm around Bill, I walk away encouraged and excited about what our generation can do to impact culture. He would argue that vision—the ability to impart hope to your team—is the greatest role of any leader.

Bill Hybels understands this leadership essential as much as any person I've ever been around. He inspires others to create a picture of the future that produces passion in people. Hybels once said something about vision that changed me forever:

> Leaders take people from here to there. A true leader must have an insane desire to leave "here" because we must move "there." Leaders have to have a desire to move from where they are now to where they need to be. It's the core message of leadership. If a leader lacks this ability to move their people from here to there, leaders should turn in their badge. People won't follow them.[2]

Our research sadly showed that less than one-quarter of Christians today feel that "their workplace has a clear vision that is easily understood by employees." We need more leaders like Nicky Gumbel and Bill Hybels, who intentionally, clearly, and regularly cast vision to their teams. We need more leaders and fewer managers.

Managers work on things that are right in front of them. They manage the e-mail inbox, respond to staff crises, sign checks, pay bills, and then drive home to relax at night before they have to do it all over again. Manage, rinse, repeat. But leaders are fixated on the next day, the next goal, the next project. While managers are tending the grass, leaders are peering over the hill. Sure, they respond to what is in front of them in the here and now, but they are also brainstorming about tomorrow. They exert energy to invent the future. Unlike a manager, a leader lives in the tension of the now and the next.

Solomon knew how important this essential is to effective leadership. The ancient king once said that people perish where vision is lacking (Proverbs 29:18). They will dry up, give up, and back up. But the opposite is also true. Where vision is present and communicated, organizations will spring to life.

YOUNG HOPEFULS

At Catalyst, we've tried to display this essential both internally and externally. Several years ago, I recognized that one of the best ways to remain hopeful and vision-centered as an organization was to fill our team with young visionaries. Though most Christians (67 percent) believe the work they are doing helps to create a better world, our research found that younger Christians are more likely to concur *strongly* with that statement.

If your organization swells with experienced and learned professionals, everyone becomes an expert. You're less likely to take risks or try new things for the organization. You're also more likely to be cynical because you've stacked your team with individuals who've experienced the world's harshest realities. Nothing will kill this essential faster than cynicism, a sense of entitlement, and a know-it-all attitude.

So whenever a position opens up on your team, consider young hopefuls—people who haven't been marred by the crushing disappointments of life. Look for individuals who still believe that the impossible is possible.

Twenty Points on Leading Twentysomethings

We gather thousands of young leaders on an annual basis, and most of our Catalyst staff members are under the age of thirty. So here are twenty ways we have learned to better lead the next generation:

1. *Give them freedom with their schedules.* I'll admit, giving young leaders freedom with their schedules is tough for me. But it creates buy in and loyalty.

2. *Provide them projects, not a career.* Careers are just not the same anymore. Young leaders desire options, just like free agents.

3. *Create a family environment.* Work, family, and social life are all intertwined for the younger generation, so make sure the work environment is experiential and family oriented. Everything is connected.

4. *Cause is important.* Tie in compassion and justice to the "normal." Causes and opportunities to give back are important.

5. *Embrace social media.* Social media is here to stay, and young leaders know how to use it.

6. *Accept that they are tech savvy.* For this generation, technology is the norm. They grew up using Xboxes, iPhones, laptops, and iPads. If you want a response, text first, then call. Or send a direct message on Twitter or a Facebook private message.

7. *Lead each person uniquely.* Don't create standards or rules that apply to everyone. Customize your approach to each young leader. (I'll admit, this one is difficult!)

8. *Make authenticity and honesty the standard for your corporate culture.* Twentysomethings tend to be cynical and don't trust someone just because they are in charge.

9. *Understand they are not interested in climbing the corporate ladder.* Today's young leaders are more concerned about making a difference and leaving their mark.

10. *Give them opportunities early with major responsibility.* They don't want to wait their turn. They want to make a difference now and will find an outlet for influence and responsibility somewhere else if you don't give it to them. Empower them early and often.

11. *Accept that they want the larger win, not the personal small gain.* Young leaders in general have an abundance mentality instead of scarcity mentality.

12. *Meet their desire for partnering and collaboration.* Twentysomethings are not interested in drawing lines. Collaboration is the new currency, along with generosity.

13. *Realize they're not about working for a personality.* This

generation isn't interested in laboring long hours to build a temporal kingdom for one person. But they will work their guts out for a cause and vision bigger than themselves.

14. *Provide opportunities for mentoring, learning, and discipleship.* Many older leaders think twentysomethings aren't interested in generational wisdom transfer. This is not true at all. Younger leaders are hungry for mentoring and discipleship, so build it into your organizational environment.

15. *Coach them and encourage them.* Young leaders want to gain wisdom through experience. Come alongside them; don't just tell them what to do.

16. *Create opportunities for quality time, individually and corporately.* Twentysomethings want to be led by example, not just by words.

17. *Hold them accountable.* This generation wants to be held accountable by those who are living out an authentic life. Measure them and give them constant feedback.

18. *Grasp that the sky is the limit in their minds.* Older leaders need to understand that younger leaders have a much broader and global perspective, which makes wowing them much more difficult.

19. *Recognize their values, not just their strengths.* It's not just about their skills. Don't use them without truly knowing them.

20. *Provide a system that creates stability.* Give younger leaders clear expectations with the freedom to succeed, and provide stability on the emotional, financial, and organizational side.

Seasoned and experienced leaders play an important role on any team as well. They'll help ground the vision and those tasked with carrying it out. There's a difference between being hopeful and being naive. You don't want to be a leader who lives in "hope-a-hope-a land," where everything is rosy all the time and you're always positive despite reality. Part of leadership is to paint the picture of what reality truly is and confront the brutal facts head-on. By balancing younger, more optimistic team members with older, more realistic team members, you'll be able to strike a crucial balance where hopefulness can thrive.

> To imagine things other than they are is the essence of hope. It is also the stuff of revolution.
> —LEONARD SWEET, AUTHOR

When Dietrich Bonhoeffer was stuck in a Nazi prison, he wrote a letter to his friend Eberhard Bethge, explaining his emotional state. Bonhoeffer said he was neither pessimistic (expecting things to worsen) nor optimistic (expecting things to improve). Instead, he said he was living by hope. He realized the realities of the situation he was facing, and this guarded him from blind optimism. But he also recognized that a sovereign God who works miracles was living inside of him, and this kept him from crippling pessimism. Living in this tension, he grew hopeful, and so we must also as leaders.

Leading in this balance will also help you scale your vision appropriately. Leaders—especially ideators and dreamers—tend to cast aggressive visions, but these visions must also be *achievable.* A realistic vision may be only for a city, or neighborhood, or a niche network. So I encourage leaders to set rigorous goals and then allow for flexibility as they test them. Scale your vision appropriately. Teams need to be challenged, but they also need to believe they can conquer the mountain you've asked them to climb.

Not every idea is going to have a global scale. You want a vision that stretches you, but not one that cannot be realistically achieved. Strive to be a hopeful visionary, not an unrealistic dreamer. Don't buy into hype-centered thinking that leans on sensationalism and inflates your goals so large that people won't take you seriously. We've all seen this with leaders who weren't willing to confront reality. A true visionary operates on hope rather than hype. A catalyst leader knows that hype produces chatter but hope inspires action.

I've observed that the most hopeful, vision-centered leaders are:

- *Optimistic about the future.* Even when sales are down or morale is low or the budget must be cut, hopeful leaders believe tomorrow holds great opportunities for personal and organizational success. They are forward-thinking, inspiring, enthusiastic, and positive, and they have a vision bigger than just what is in front of them.

• *Focused on the best in their people, not the worst.* Hopeful leaders are encouraging. Rather than browbeat their team over yesterday's failures, they focus on the unique strengths of every employee.

• *Never satisfied, but always content.* Hopeful leaders are always moving toward a goal, but they don't allow it to steal their joy. They seem happy where they are but refuse to stay there.

• *Consumed with making tomorrow better than today.* Hopeful leaders never settle. They know there are mountains to climb and a vision to carry out, and they see each day as an opportunity to improve and grow. Give your team reason to believe that tomorrow is filled with greatness waiting to be realized.

• *Accepting of change.* Hopeful leaders embrace change in their lives and organizations because they know this is often the fastest path to growth and improvement. They have a "bring it on" attitude and invite change with open arms. They are innovative and try new things at the risk of failing.

• *Inclusive, not exclusive.* Hopeful leaders invite others into their vision. They are confident of where they are going, and are able to get others involved and bought in. People won't willingly follow you until they can see how they share in the future you envision.

- *Personally bought in.* Hopeful leaders have a vision that propels them personally. It stirs them up and drives them forward. They don't wait on someone else to hand them a vision, and they don't need to draft one with pen and paper; it's already inside them.

The above list describes the type of leader we seek to hire, develop, and sustain at Catalyst. But it also describes the type of leader we want to cultivate in our community. So we attempt to remain positive at our events, not railing against what's wrong with the world but showcasing what's right. If people leave a Catalyst event angry or frustrated about culture or life, we have failed. We want our participants to leave energized and excited and dreaming about how good the culture can be with hard work and God's help.

In fact, we even want this essential from our larger "family" of volunteers who are part of helping make Catalyst events among the best in the world: the part-time staff and volunteers who help create our experiences and truly make us who we are. I love when they have as much excitement, energy, and hope in our vision as our paid staff does. I love to hear our volunteers talk about "our event" rather than "your event." When your organizational vision causes those who aren't paid to be consumed by it, that's a good sign. You want people who are not part of the team to begin to buy in. You want everyone involved using words like *we* and *us* instead of *you*. Look for people like this. Hopeful leaders create hopeful cultures that create hopeful organizations that constantly release vision copycats. Team members who take on, embody, and live out the mission and vision of their leader, and ultimately their organization, way more powerfully and courageously than the leader ever could.

One of the ways we know we are truly catalyst leaders is if we are helping others around us flourish. Leaders help others flourish; they don't hold others back.

Ten Morale Killers to Avoid with Your Team
http://catalystleader.com/moralekillers

ENVIRONMENTS OF HOPE

Catalyst leaders want to create environments that foster hope, because hope will outlive all other attributes we might nurture. After all, hope is one of the three forces in this world—faith, hope, and love—that will remain when we have nothing else left (1 Corinthians 13:13). Because of its permanence, hope can make a difference and change the world. Catalyst's attendees know this is one of our goals even if they haven't heard it clearly communicated.

Many years ago, a speaker at one of our Catalyst events decided to use his time to rant against modern Christianity. Much of what he said was true, but it didn't sit well with our participants. Why? Because they didn't expect a critical spirit at our event. They came to be inspired and equipped and encouraged. Our speaker was engaging in a conversation that needed to be had, but our event wasn't the venue in which to have it. We feel called to create space where hope—not cynicism, skepticism, or negativism—grows.[3]

One of the ways we carry out this vision is to showcase the best movements taking place among Christians and giving our participants an opportunity to join in. For example, we've championed adoption over the last few years. Over 143 million orphans live on our planet today. A couple of years ago, Catalyst decided to partner with organizations that were addressing the orphan crisis—410 Bridge, Compassion, Bethany Christian Services, Adoption Journey, and Never Ending Hope—to promote the hopeful vision that the church could eradicate the orphan crisis. We launched www.143million.org to get the word out, and showcased ways our community could get involved. As a result, we've seen incredible progress within the networks connected to Catalyst, and our team has heard from at least 150 people just in our circle and community who've started the adoption process as a result of this effort.

These are the types of initiatives we want Catalyst connected to. Inspiring projects. Innovative solutions. Forward-thinking ideas for how the world can move closer to Jesus' kingdom vision. We believe all two billion Christians have been called to care for orphans and widows (James 1:27). At

SHARE ON 🐦 f
Hopeful leaders create hopeful cultures that create hopeful organizations. #CatalystLeader

the nexus of these two figures is an opportunity for change and a reason to hope.

We want to move the needle on this issue to make a difference and, in the process, inspire hope and a sense that we can accomplish something bigger than ourselves. We want to motivate a generation to remain positive and change the lives of children and families.

> If your vision doesn't compel, move or stir people, your vision is too small.
> —CRAIG GROESCHEL, PASTOR OF LIFECHURCH.TV

I love the story of Riley Goodfellow, a nine-year-old we highlighted at an event a few years ago. She ate rice and beans for a month to understand what children in developing nations may experience, and she raised ten thousand dollars for charity:water during the process. She had no corporate budget. No devoted team. Nothing. She accomplished it all with a simple vision for how she could impact the world.

This is the kind of spirit we want to spread through Catalyst. We want to cultivate leaders who create possibilities rather than make excuses. Influencers who are willing to move outside their comfort zones. Change makers who dream about accomplishing projects so big that even their closest friends think them crazy. A catalyst leader knows that God can accomplish what seems impossible to us.

STEP UP

I'm not always the hopeful visionary leader I should be. I can get so focused on today's tasks that I lose sight of tomorrow's vision. I can lose myself in the logistics of an event—bogged down in my to-do list—and fail to provide energy for my team by painting a picture of what success looks like. In these moments, I find myself being pulled along by the energy, vision, and excitement of team members and key volunteers. As leaders, it's our responsibility to step up, cast vision, and lead with courage even when immediate pressures suffocate us.

Twelve Ways to Step Out of Your Comfort Zone
http://catalystleader.com/comfortzone

Get outside your comfort zone. Dream about accomplishing a project so out of your abilities that it keeps you up at night. God calls us to think big. So what's on your heart or stirring in you that you keep pushing back because it doesn't seem possible? Pursue it. God can accomplish what seems impossible to us.

We realize that people won't willingly follow you until they can see the role they play in the future you envision. When you are optimistic, enthusiastic, and energetic, your team and those you serve will be too. That's why I believe hopefulness is an essential of the catalyst leader. When you give people a reason to believe that tomorrow can be better than yesterday, they'll be inspired to make the most of today.

I'm incredibly hopeful and optimistic that over the next twenty years we can make a difference and change an entire generation. A new generation of leaders is ready to take the reins. We all must have vision and passion and be leaders others want to follow. We have to be constantly and relentlessly in pursuit of what *ought* to be—in hopeful anticipation of that which will come to be—painting a picture of what's next. Leaders who others want to follow have a vision that is inspiring and powerful. As I discovered in Africa with Compassion International, there's nothing quite like creating a hopeful picture of the future to produce tremendous passion in people.

SHARE ON 🐦 f
Dream about accomplishing a project so out of your abilities that it keeps you up at night. God calls us to think big. #CatalystLeader

FIVE HOPEFUL LEADERS YOU SHOULD KNOW

- ## TYLER WIGG-STEVENSON | TWO FUTURES PROJECT

  Nine countries in the world possess more than ten thousand nuclear weapons, each one capable of vast and indiscriminate killing. Abolishing these weapons is a daunting task, but Tyler believes it is both possible and necessary. He launched the Two Futures Project to engage the issue by mobilizing and educating Christians, and since then, he's become a sought-after voice on the issue.

- ## JENA LEE NARDELLA | BLOOD:WATER MISSION

  Confronting either the AIDS crisis or the global water crisis is a massive undertaking, but trying to tackle them both requires chutzpah. Yet Jena and her team, fueled by their hope for a better future, have done exactly that. Discovering a vital link between the two crises, they're working hard to eliminate both.

- ## BECKY STRAW | THE ADVENTURE PROJECT

  As cofounder and chief adventurist of the Adventure Project, Becky is intent on giving hope to entrepreneurs and social innovators by supporting social enterprises and projects around the world. She believes in the power of giving jobs that create dignity and worth in others, and ultimately transforms communities. Her enthusiasm is inspiring and contagious!

- ## TIM AND BECKY O'MARA | BELTLINE BIKE SHOP

  In 2008, Tim and Becky O'Mara found out that a bicycle could be more than just a mode of transportation; it's also a vehicle for relationship building. Today, they operate the Beltline Bike Shop nestled in a diverse neighborhood in southwest Atlanta. Kids earn bikes through community service. While they utilize the shop to keep their bikes functioning, they're also building relationships with positive adult role models in their neighborhood.

- ## JUSTIN DILLON | SLAVERY FOOTPRINT

  With estimates of up to twenty million people living in slavery, some might say working to eliminate that problem is too ambitious. But not Justin. Through the innovative Slavery Footprint project, he created a way to calculate how you are supporting slavery through your current lifestyle. Thousands of people are now working to reduce their slavery footprint, using the free market to free slaves around the world.

8

COLLABORATIVE

DRAW POWER FROM PARTNERS

Refuse to do anything less than collaborate with people as you lead. Pull other people's leadership into play.
—NANCY ORTBERG, CATALYST WEST

EVERY STRONG LEADER I'VE MET SHARES AT LEAST ONE DESIRE: to grow. Leaders want to improve and expand their reach and influence. I've never met an effective leader of an organization who says, "I think we're about as successful as we need to be. I've decided we should just coast from now on." But progress has a price tag. When your organization achieves a certain size or level of success, you'll begin to experience a whole slate of problems you've never encountered before.

For an organization that is as successful and as large as

Catalyst, one of the greatest temptations we face is to make everything about us. We fight the desire to engage in self-promotion and self-glorification, knowing all the while that no matter how well we execute a project, it is God who deserves the credit.

Many organizations operate like this; they are like a statue standing on a roundabout in the middle of a city. It has been built for all to see, to admire, to pay homage to. But our team purposed early on to never become a statue. Instead, we want to be like the road system around that statue. We want to connect people, move people, transport people where they need to go, and introduce them to places and other people they might never have encountered otherwise.

Not long ago, our team grew concerned with the global clean water crisis. More than 1.2 billion people worldwide lack access to clean drinking water, resulting in millions of deaths each year. We decided to address this issue in a collaborative way by connecting the Catalyst community to the problem through a partnership with Living Water International. Our collaborative efforts raised close to three million dollars.

This type of collaboration has become our model. When Joplin, Missouri, was ravaged by tornadoes, we worked with Venture Expeditions to raise one hundred thousand dollars for storm victims by doing a bike tour from Joplin to Atlanta. The final destination was the arena in which our event was taking place.

We partnered with Hope International one year to

promote microfinance by giving all thirteen thousand attendees at our Atlanta event ten dollars and challenging them to multiply it. And it doesn't stop with Hope International. We currently partner with more than one hundred organizations and have more than seventy-five denominations connected to Catalyst. Organizations such as Compassion International, charity:water, First Response Team of America, One Day's Wages, International Justice Mission, Hoops of Hope, the A21 Campaign, and many others have been profiled at our events. At Catalyst, we want to be a big tent that aggregates and unifies leaders from all different backgrounds and continually expands the circle wider. Untold numbers of lives have been changed by these collaborative efforts.

Collaboration is integral for leaders moving forward. It is part of the framework for trading equity and value in today's economy. Collaboration is now the norm, not the exception. A catalyst leader wants to work together with all kinds of leaders and organizations, without worrying who gets the credit.

Our Catalyst team doesn't want to construct walls; we want to build bridges. And we're motivated by our conviction that a platform can either be selfishly stockpiled, or it can be shared with others. We want the Catalyst platform to be the machinery that lifts others up. Rather than promote our organization, we want to elevate people, causes, and organizations we feel are worthy. As a result, we've become a launching pad for a mosaic of voices spanning denominations, theological perspectives, races, and even generations.

COMMITTING TO COLLABORATION

At Catalyst we've tried to be an example of working with people we may not agree with for the common good of everyone. This is different than many networks, communities, and event-driven organizations in existence today who attempt to only affiliate with those who think and believe like they do. If there is another organization with different beliefs than ours but a common vision with common goals, we'll consider partnering with them. Our vision is to be inclusive, not exclusive. We believe everyone can contribute as long as we find a common foundation. We desire to be known by what we are for, not by what we are against. That is where unity starts. In the case of the church, Jesus is the common denominator. Lots of organizations and leaders can rally and unify and work together around Jesus.

The culture of partnerships we have created has taught us at least three positive effects of collaboration:

- *Collaboration creates innovation.* By surrounding yourself with various perspectives, your team will be introduced to ideas and systems they might never encounter otherwise. This will often lead to fresh thinking and better solutions within your own organization.
- *Collaboration reduces unnecessary risk.* In a partnership, the success and credit are shared with others.

But the risk is too. There is a joint investment of time, resources, and brainpower that reduces risk. If a collaborative project ends up falling flat, each partner shoulders only a portion of the losses, financial and otherwise.

• *Collaboration amplifies success.* A simple rule drives collaboration: more input leads to more output. When you convene more innovators and leaders, you'll gather more ideas and have more hands to carry them out. When you pool resources, you'll have a larger pot to propel the project forward. As a result, partnerships often amplify success beyond what a single team might otherwise achieve, resulting in a win/win.

Our commitment to collaboration has even led our team to partner with competing organizations. We've promoted and endorsed multiple conferences at our Catalyst events because we believe in the work they are doing and know it will be helpful for leaders at all levels. Of course, some people may choose to attend those conferences instead of ours the next year.

SHARE ON
When you collaborate with other innovators and leaders, you'll gather more ideas and have more hands to carry them out. #CatalystLeader

Our team recognizes the risk, but our commitment to a collaborative culture overcomes any worries. It also allows us to take the energy we would have spent on protecting our turf and reinvest it into making our events the best they can be. The power of us moving in the same direction overcomes any downside to guarding our territory and hoarding our community.

We were inspired to take collaboration more seriously in 2008 when we partnered with author Seth Godin for the release of his book *Tribes: We Need You to Lead Us* (Penguin, 2008). He had been exploring the subject of collaboration for two decades, so the book's topic intrigued our team. In an effort to embody the message of the book, we gave away thirteen thousand copies of his book, a month before it released, to all who attended our Atlanta event. The collaborative effort created a win for Seth and for the Catalyst community too.

> You don't have to blow out someone else's candle to make yours shine brighter.

A catalyst leader works together with all kinds of leaders and organizations, and ultimately doesn't care who gets the credit. Some people would rather throw rocks and grenades than life preservers, but the rules of engagement have changed in today's culture. Catalyst leaders desire to set a different example. No more lone rangers.

Many people see organizational leadership like running a race. Some influencers attempt to trip those who start to pass them, fueled by the fear that another's advance could be their demise. At Catalyst, we cheer others on as they race alongside us, recognizing that those we often view as competitors are actually teammates. Those leaders and organizations might pass us up, and that's okay. Their success makes us all better.

Best-selling author Don Miller experienced collaboration up close recently, when the feature film *Blue Like Jazz*, based on Miller's book, was saved through a Kickstarter online campaign that raised hundreds of thousands of dollars to keep the film going and ultimately showing in theaters across the country. Don and our mutual friend Bob Goff talked at Catalyst West about the concept of "with"—a lifelong strategy of working on things together with folks you like. Community is oxygen for our souls. We all want to be part of, to be "with," something bigger than ourselves.

If you desire to advance your level of leadership, one of the best things you can do is to build bridges with two kinds of organizations. The first should be an entity that is in the same line of work, but not a direct competitor. The second should be an entity that you have profound philosophical differences with. Set up a collaborative meeting between their team and yours. Share best practices and brainstorm together about projects your respective teams are working on. When the meetings conclude, I bet your team will thank you, and you'll all be convinced the time was well spent.

The next best thing to being wise oneself is to live in a circle of those who are.

—C. S. LEWIS, AUTHOR

Christians haven't always been good at this. We have a tendency to huddle with a narrow group of like-minded individuals. But I think this can be a very unhealthy practice for leaders. When a catalyst leader's team associates with an organization he or she might not interact with otherwise, the leader builds relationships with those who hold different perspectives. These become iron-sharpening-iron relationships that challenge and almost always strengthen leaders. For example, we've partnered with the White House Faith Outreach Office on adoption, foster care, and the issue of fatherlessness, even though many of our team members differ with the administration's public policy. Most will tell you this partnership has grown and stretched them.

One word of caution: collaboration requires clarity. Make sure expectations are explained and agreed upon on the front end. As a collaborative friend often reminds me, "Good contracts make good partnerships." Outline boundaries, responsibilities, and what a win looks like. You may love the idea of a handshake agreement, but the hand that shakes can also slap. It's easier to outline expectations of collaboration at the outset than in the midst of a disagreement. So collaborate freely, but collaborate cautiously.

GIVE BIG

Collaboration is built on generosity, which is a new currency in our culture. Generosity wins. We continue to move toward open source, generosity, shared influence, relational networks, shared platforms, content partnerships, and collaborative projects. The most influential platforms today revolve around sharing and generosity.

The Catalyst community learned this from Jack Dorsey, the founder of Twitter, who joined us at Catalyst West for an in-depth interview. He confirmed that the power of Twitter is generosity, sharing, and providing value to others. According to Dorsey, many of the revolutionary aspects of Twitter were invented by leaders outside the company from the larger Twitter-user community—things such as the @ symbol, hashtag, retweet, trending topic, search mechanism, and even the word *tweet* itself.

Dorsey believes in the power of a team and a community working together for something significant to happen. According to Dorsey, "Technology is a tool. And it's only great when it makes us more human. Being human means doing good things. [Twitter] should foster approachability and a better world, and help in doing good. Twitter at its best connects people instantly to the things that matter most."[1]

Those who have the greatest influence within social media channels are the ones willing to put others above themselves and collaborate well. Leaders today have resources such as Twitter, Facebook, LinkedIn, YouTube, Flickr, Instagram, and many more social media tools that make constant sharing and partnering readily available.

What Poisons a Team Quickly
http://catalystleader.com/poisonsateam

One of the best examples of a collaborative organization is LifeChurch.tv. They freely give their resources to thousands of churches around the world through their "Open Network." Craig Groeschel, Bobby Gruenewald, and the entire LifeChurch team do an incredible job of collaborating and seeing their church's vision in partnership with others, both in their community and around the world. It's about the greater cause. They know that fulfilling their calling does not mean building their own empire, but working toward something greater.

Collaboration isn't easy, and it almost always requires sacrifice, both personally and organizationally. Perhaps this is why our research found that 39 percent of Christian leaders believe collaboration is one of the most important leadership traits of the next decade, but only 15 percent say this essential best describes them. In order to collaborate, you and your team will have to compromise and may even have to give up something you value. Those who choose this path must nurture the virtue of generosity and learn the art of placing others' interests above their own. This is not a natural way to work and will require practice. But such is the way of collaboration.

We were all taught to share when we were young (though many of us never learned), but as leaders, it's imperative that we are willing to share. We need to discover the art of influence through giving more than receiving. At Catalyst, we try to give more than we receive, both personally among our staff and professionally as an organization.

As a result, we want everyone to win if possible. We want to create wins for our individual Catalyst team members and the entire organization. But we also want our partners to win. The paradox of collaboration is that when you help others succeed, you almost always create a win for yourself in the process. Ultimately, partnering well means combining efforts to achieve something greater than what can be done separate or apart from each other. It's about creating win/win situations. A higher tide really will lift all boats.

CARROTS AND STICKS

Dov Seidman is CEO of LRN, a consulting company that helps leading companies like Pfizer, Apple, and Viacom improve their corporate culture. He was named one of the "Top 60 Global Thinkers of the Last Decade" by the *Economic Times* and is author of the best-selling book *HOW: Why How We Do Anything Means Everything*. Seidman has observed profound changes taking place in America's workplace as a result of globalization, democratization, and the increased availability of information. And as the old system fades away, he says, companies and their leaders cannot continue to operate as they have in the past if they want to thrive.

"The old system of 'command and control'—using carrots and sticks—to exert power *over* people is fast being replaced by 'connect and collaborate'—to generate power *through* people," Seidman argues.

We at Catalyst recognize the truth in his perspective, and so have many of today's foremost Christian leaders.

A Lifetime of Leading Well: Peb Jackson

For almost fifteen years, Peb Jackson has been a mentor to me. He's taught me about faith, friendship, and leadership. But perhaps the most profound lesson I've gleaned from Peb is the importance of collaboration and generosity.

As the principal of Jackson Consulting Group, Peb has made a living by building networks of organizations from all sectors of society. His clients work in public policy, community development, media, education, and philanthropy. He's helped launch influential organizations, worked with leaders such as Rick Warren, raised millions of dollars to support ministries like Young Life, and even produced feature films.

He sits on more than half a dozen boards, and though you might not know him, many influential leaders keep Peb on speed dial.

But the ability to collaborate across lines of interest and connect those who might otherwise never meet comes naturally to Peb. He pays close attention to knowing who is in front of him and who that person might benefit from knowing. He connects people to people, people to projects, and projects to partners. Unlike self-serving networkers, Peb cares about the friends he serves. It's his lifetime calling and purpose to be a connector and help make introductions and bring different leaders together. Peb lives out the idea of "more together than on our own." His personal agendas are less important than meeting the needs of the connected community he has created. His inquisitive spirit, willingness to serve, and focus on others make Peb a model collaborator for a new generation of leaders.

PITCH A WIDE TENT

Churches seem to resist the collaborative spirit most of all. Often third-party organizations or even other churches in the area are better equipped to meet the needs or perform functions for that church. Perhaps another congregation has been running a student summer camp for many years, or a local homeless outreach center is working to care for the needs of the poor. One local church could easily partner with the work another local church is already performing, but fears creep in among church leaders that members may end up giving some of their tithes to that organization instead of to the church. Or the church staff worries that students may like the partner church better and transfer. So instead of partnering with another church, the local church hires additional staff, creates a new program, and reinvents the proverbial wheel.

Occasionally, I encounter an exception to this system, and it gives me hope. When Andy Stanley and North Point Community Church decided to launch their fifth satellite location, they chose Duluth, Georgia, as its home. Like many new church plants, Gwinnett Church was forced to meet in community space at the local civic center. While the facility met their needs, setting up and tearing down equipment each Sunday strained their volunteer team and separated them from their families most of the day.

That's when James Merritt, pastor of Cross Pointe Church, reached out to Jeff Henderson, Gwinnett Church's campus pastor. Even though Cross Pointe was less than a quarter of mile from the civic center and had many reasons to view the new church as a competitor, Merritt saw a kingdom opportunity. Since Cross Pointe met in the mornings and Gwinnett met in the evenings, Merritt offered Cross Pointe's facilities to the Gwinnett church family. Gwinnett Church accepted, and the congregations formed a collaborative partnership. Today, these two churches with separate leadership teams are thriving alongside each other in the same community. They are collaborating rather than competing, and they see each other as partners rather than rivals.

"We talk a big game, but there is so much competition out there and there is so much pastoral jealousy out there," Merritt told his congregation. "It's time that someone stood up and showed the world how churches can cooperate and families can come together. We are either going to be kingdom minded or we're not."

John 13 outlines the essence of biblical collaboration. The world will know us by our love. The church working together and unified is an unstoppable force. We've seen this with many partnerships with Catalyst. We want Catalyst to be a big tent gatherer that provides a safe environment for leaders from all backgrounds, perspectives, and denominations. We want to unite, not divide. And we require our community of young leaders to be willing to work together.

This is the kind of spirit we want to propagate at Catalyst events. In 2011, we received a letter from a participant following an event. He and his wife had planted a church in North Carolina, and after our event they felt led to champion orphan care in their community. They had to choose between launching their own ministry and partnering with others who had decades of experience in this sort of work. The former might produce a big win for their new congregation—perhaps even springboard them into prominence—but the latter made more sense. They'd witnessed the collaborative spirit in which we'd worked on the issue and decided to pursue a similar model.

"We arrived at Catalyst as church planters trying to genuinely build a church community. We left with a completely different perspective," the pastor wrote. "I am much more interested now in sparking a movement as opposed to building a church."

They partnered with Compassion International, Bethany Christian Services, and their local Department of Social Services to address the needs of orphans in their community. Their church screened a video on adoption on "Orphan Care Sunday," and mobilized many to address the problem. The church wasn't featured in any magazines for launching a flashy ministry, but they were able to achieve more good in the lives of children than they would have otherwise.

Catalyst desires to be an organization in which leaders from all backgrounds, perspectives, denominations, and theological leanings can gather. It doesn't matter if you are a liberal Episcopal priest or conservative Southern Baptist pastor, a manager of a nonprofit or the president of a large company, a retiree who spends her days volunteering or college student who just wants to follow Jesus—we want Catalyst to be a safe and stimulating space.

The reasoning behind our collaborative philosophy is our belief that safe spaces are essential for trust. And trust is required for collaboration. "If I had to pick the one thing to get right about any collaborative effort, I would choose trust," writes author Larry Prusak in *Harvard Business Review*. "More than incentives, technology, roles, missions, or structures, it is trust that makes collaboration really work. There can be collaboration without it, but it won't be very productive or sustainable in the long run."[2] If a new generation of catalyst leaders is going to partner in the pursuit of a common cause, we must construct a big tent in which they can connect with each other and dream together.

Here are a few keys for collaboration and building bridges, based on conversations with Charles Lee, the founder of Ideation Conference and a great practitioner of collaboration and partnership:

1. *Make sure expectations are clearly laid out on the front end.* Good contracts make good partnerships. Good fences make good neighbors. Many times we don't take time to spell out all the details of a partnership in full disclosure. It is crucial to put everything on paper, in an agreement, and make sure all the details are understood. Define the wins, and create clear expectations and agreements. Make sure all parties involved are clear on what is expected and what looks like success.

2. *Stay adaptive, humble, and accessible.* Flexibility is key when it comes to partnerships. Build everything on trust. Being human, approachable, transparent, and authentic makes collaboration

much easier and more effective. Be a great listener, ask more questions, and figure out ways to serve.

3. *See collaboration as a need, not just an option.* Collaboration is incredibly important in today's economy. Success depends on it. Combining strengths of two organizations makes for a powerful force. It's messy, but it can work. Creativity comes out of great collaboration.

4. *Choose wisely.* Everything today is now recorded and made public. So be careful. It's much easier to say no on the front end to a potential partnership or collaborative project than it is to unravel a partnership gone bad. Good partnerships start with a deep knowledge of the other.

5. *Be intentional in finding common areas of interest and connection.* Intentionality is crucial, for both crafting the partnership as well as making it happen. Intentionality requires you to follow up, probably again and again.

6. *Make connections.* Great collaborators are always connecting friends within their circles. The ultimate value of these connections is not for you; it's for others. Be others-focused.

How to Celebrate Your "Rivals"
http://catalystleader/celebraterivals

COLLABORATION ON THE INSIDE

Before you can build a culture of interorganizational collaboration, you need to build a culture of intraorganizational collaboration. Organizations need to open up communication lines and learn to share information with each other across departments. Lew Platt, the former CEO of Hewlett-Packard, once said, "If HP knew what HP knows, we would be three times more productive."[3] Often an organization's greatest limitation is its inability to connect its employees with other employees working within earshot of each other.

In years past, many American companies and nonprofits were organized in a strict hierarchy. As more employees were added, the organizational chart grew longer, not wider. But that trend is shifting as emerging leaders are looking to work *with* others, in addition to working *for* others.

Dov Seidman notes:

> As power shifts to individuals, leadership itself must shift with it—from coercive or motivational leadership that uses sticks or carrots to extract performance and allegiance *out* of people to inspirational leadership that inspires commitment and innovation and hope *in* people.

At Catalyst, we've attempted to flatten our organizational structure. We've done this by streamlining communication and having an open-door policy. Team members can directly approach anyone else if they have a problem that involves that person or need to get their opinion on a project. They aren't forced to climb a chain of command. Our decision-making is pushed out across the organization rather than always dictated from the top down.

> You can do what I cannot do. I can do what you cannot do. Together we can do great things.
> —MOTHER TERESA

When I discuss Catalyst's efforts to move from a hierarchical structure to a flat organizational structure in an effort to motivate other leaders to do the same, I often sense consternation and anxiety from those leaders. I gather that some are scared of implementing such reforms because it would mean a loss of control. In fact, that is exactly what it would require. But our experience has been that such a corporate culture best focuses a team on organization-sized wins rather than on small personal gains. It promotes "us" and "we" over "you" and "me."

Why Your Leadership Must Be Social
http://catalystleader.com/socialleadership

Additionally, when individuals achieve a win, the entire team celebrates. This creates an open-source environment, where we feel comfortable giving away ideas rather than protecting or hoarding them. An organization with closefisted employees who are always trying to climb a hierarchical ladder will never be as healthy as a collaborative one in which ideas are freely shared. This partnering mentality is catching on across industries. Many of the new-economy companies create environments where everyone is working in the same room. No corner offices, no plush closed-door environments, just open, collaborative work space that encourages everyone to work together.

Open-source collaboration has quickly caught on in the technology realm. A great example of this is the way that programmers and developers are creating open-source apps for the Android phone through the Google platform. This open-source mentality is about giving away one's ideas for the better.[4] Their work is not about protecting or hoarding. It's about giving away as much as possible so that everyone benefits. Leaders must do likewise, learning to steward rather than to control their platforms. The more influence you have, the more intentional you have to be about giving it away.

In some ways, we've torn a page out of the Pixar playbook at Catalyst. Pixar taps into the power of comedy improv. If you've seen improv, you know that it requires working in conjunction with others to make the moment better. You have to build on someone else's idea. Randy Nelson, dean of Pixar University, talks about the power of improv as it relates to lessons they've learned at Pixar. "Two core principles of improv have always guided us. The first: accept every offer. You don't know where things are going, but if you don't accept the offer, it's going nowhere. You either have a dead-end or a possibility, and we teach to take the possibility. The second principle: make your partner look good. Always take the chance to 'plus' someone on your team. Make them look good. Everyone should be focused on making other team-mates and partners look good."[5] At Pixar, this means taking a piece of work and not immediately judging it or trying to fix it, but adding to it and making it better.

Philippians 2:2–5 inspires me personally, and also com-pels us as an organization:

> Make my joy complete by being of the same mind, main-taining the same love, united in spirit, intent on one purpose. Do nothing from selfishness or empty conceit, but with humility of mind regard one another as more impor-tant than yourselves. Do not merely look out for your own personal interests, but also for the interests of others. Have this attitude in yourselves, which was also in Christ Jesus.

Do you want to grow, improve, and expand your lead-ership? Then seek to rid your organization of internal and external selfishness. Don't merely look out for your own interests, but rather find partners in whom your team can invest. You will encounter problems along the way, but the dividends you'll reap by nurturing a collaborative environ-ment will far exceed any price you have to pay. We can do far more together than we can alone.

FIVE COLLABORATIVE LEADERS YOU SHOULD KNOW

- CLAIRE DIAZ-ORTIZ | TWITTER

  Claire is focused on connecting leaders in the social space. As the social innovation director at Twitter, she helps connect causes, influencers, organizations, and projects to the platform of Twitter. She's a natural connector and makes sure that connections are valuable for all involved.

- BETHANY HOANG | INTERNATIONAL JUSTICE MISSION

  An advocate for human rights, Bethany regularly convenes and equips leaders in all sectors to help bring justice to the forefront. As the director of the International Justice Mission Institute for Biblical Justice, she helps engage with the biblical call to seek justice on behalf of the global poor suffering from oppression, and speaks at churches, conferences, and universities to bring a greater awareness in the pursuit of global justice.

- CHARLES LEE | IDEATION CONFERENCE

  Charles Lee is a true collaborator. His Ideation conferences create myriad connections that are built on partnership and working together. Charles is deeply connected in all kinds of niches, networks, and industries, and he has favor and influence across many genres and networks.

- ## DAVE BLANCHARD AND JOSH KWAN | PRAXIS

  Dave and Josh founded Praxis as a way to build knowledge and networks for innovators who want to launch new projects. Built on a spirit of collaboration, they select "fellows," or social entrepreneurs, who have strong ideas and connect them with mentors and resources to help their dreams become reality.

- ## BLAKE CANTERBURY | BEREMEDY

  Collaboration is about more than networking; it can be the engine for accomplishing good in the world. Blake founded BeRemedy to use social media to connect those in need to those who can help. Through applications like Twitter and Facebook, BeRemedy alerts users when someone in their community needs help. Members then respond or pass the message on to those who can.

CONCLUSION

MOVING FORWARD, LOOKING BACK

ALMOST A DECADE AFTER I FOUND MYSELF COUNTING CEILING tiles with the weight of the organization resting on my shoulders, my heart is full. Leading Catalyst has provided me with opportunities to grow and develop as a leader, and more importantly, the chance to help develop a new generation of change makers who give me great hope about the future of the Christian movement. And along the way, I've had some serious fun.

I've rapped with one of my childhood music icons, Rev Run from Run DMC. I've listened to my dad and former football coach talk shop with Super Bowl champion Tony Dungy. I've hung out with Eugene Peterson one afternoon after completing my devotions in his *Message* translation that morning. I've interviewed the founder of Twitter, Jack

Dorsey, who is reshaping social media as we know it. I've been able to present the Catalyst Lifetime Achievement Award to heroes of mine like Dr. John Perkins and Geoffrey Canada. And I shot a spoof video with skateboard legend Tony Hawk. Each unforgettable moment has been accentuated by the realization that those we often idolize are human like the rest of us.

But the greatest joy of my last decade isn't meeting celebrities or hanging out with best-selling authors. My joy is the friendships I've built with vendors, partners, attendees, speakers, and team members. Those who've become counselors who provide me with spiritual and professional guidance when I need it most. Men and women who pray with me and for me. I've been blessed beyond measure.

Looking back over my leadership journey so far, I'm overcome with the realization that I've still not arrived. I still feel the weight of responsibility as strongly now as I did when I first settled into this role. For every fun moment, there have been a dozen difficult ones. Times when I've been forced to make hard decisions. Sleepless nights spent wondering how I could deliver on promises I'd made.

Like many leaders, some days I long to return to the early years. To days when life was easier and simpler as the foreman at Lost Valley Ranch. When riding a horse through the Pike National Forest seemed to be the only item on the agenda. Those were times when I didn't have to worry as much about budgets, bottom lines, staffing, and growth as I do now. I'd wake up, sip some coffee, and then head out on a peaceful horseback ride in the Colorado mountains.

I never knew what a new day would bring at Lost Valley. I remember three occasions when a guest was taking a ride and his horse died midstep, spilling the guest onto a mountain path. "Leave the horse and save the guest" was our motto, much to the shock of the rider. Another time we had a guest who had traveled from England. Totally oblivious to Western ranch culture, she came down to the corral one morning dressed in chaps wearing nothing but her underwear. Gaping mouths hung all around as I informed her that chaps were supposed to be worn over blue jeans.

Over the five years I was at Lost Valley, I made some epic memories. But none surpasses my time with my mentor and the ranch's founder, Bob Foster. I was twenty-five and he was seventy-five. He knew a little something about mentoring. After all, he had been mentored by Dawson Trotman, founder of the Navigators, and legendary Dallas Theological Seminary professor Howard Hendricks. Though I didn't recognize it at that time, I now realize I was a part of a robust and honorable mentoring lineage.

Every Thursday morning, Bob Foster and I would have breakfast at his personal table on the south porch of the dining room. It overlooked the corral, and I'd often gaze at the snow-capped mountains in the distance. We'd pray together, memorize Scripture, and study the Bible, and he'd share lessons he'd learned throughout his life.

Bob had seen a lot in his day. He'd been born in the Roaring Twenties, lived through the Great Depression, and experienced the heartache of World War II. He had grown into a well-respected Christian leader, developing deep personal relationships with people like evangelist Billy Graham, World Vision founder Bob Pierce, and author Chuck Swindoll. I, on the other hand, was born in the disco era and my most significant relationship was, well, with him. Though a deep chasm had separated us, I still felt close to him on those misty, chilly early mornings.

I can still picture Bob sitting there with his cowboy hat tilted to the side at an almost comical angle. He'd bite his lip, think for a moment, and then pour out wisdom. He constantly reminded me that my twenties would establish my seventies. Bob knew that life was a series of building blocks laid early on, and he challenged me to live and lead well. He would offer homespun advice on discipline and provided accountability. The memories remind me of H. L. Mencken's words: "The best teacher is not the one who knows most but the one who is most capable of reducing knowledge to that simple compound of the obvious and wonderful."

Much of my work and life philosophy today, as well as my spiritual maturity, was crafted on those mornings. And when days get tough, I long to be back there. But, of course, I can't return to those porch-top breakfasts. Life only moves in one direction: forward. Yet I hold dear the lessons Bob gave me, including the importance of listening to those who've come before me.

Now I'm a translator, a unifier between the wise sages and the young upstarts. Bridging the gap between generations, and bringing together the older men and women leaders who have a lot of wisdom to give, and the twenty- and thirty-somethings who desire to learn from someone who has already walked the roads they now are walking.

Sadly, few leaders today are tapping the great well of wisdom found in a mentor. According to our research, only 16 percent firmly assert that they interact regularly with an older mentor who helps them navigate professional issues. Too many young leaders think they know more than their elders. They've been swept up in their own press clippings, when they really need to sit down, stop talking, and listen. We need to open our ears to the wise mentors in our lives, in our companies, in our organizations, in our families, and in our churches. We need to listen to the leaders who know both the thrill of victory and the agony of defeat, who've weathered recessions and prosperity, who've actually watched technology advance, who don't just talk about experience but have actually acquired it. More young leaders need to put down the microphone for a moment and pick up a pen and paper and start taking notes.

If you're in your twenties or thirties, find someone much older than you who can pour into your life. Be aware of those around you who know more than you do, who have experienced more than you have in life. Give them permission to speak into your life, and then open your ears and heart to what they share.

If you're an older leader, you can't just sit around and wait to be asked. You need to pursue younger leaders to invest in like Bob Foster pursued me and invested in me. You need to seek to understand, to train, to inspire, to connect, and then to release younger leaders to pursue their callings. The wisdom and experience you hold doesn't do anyone good if it remains bottled up. It must be poured out.

Every leader—regardless of age—should have at least one mentor and should be mentoring at least one other person. A twenty-year-old can invest in a twelve-year-old while a forty-year-old invests in him. And a thirty-year-old can invest in an eighteen-year-old while a fifty-year-old invests in her. You are never too old or too young to participate in the mentoring process. You need to both find and become a mentor. Remember and honor those who've helped you get to where you are. Your legacy is not only determined by what you do as you get old but also by who you are when you're young. Leading well means starting well. Building a foundation for influence now.

My heart continues to fill with hope for this generation of leaders. Leaders like you. Sure, you have faults and weaknesses like everyone else. But you also have great and untapped potential. If you can develop the eight essentials laid out in the preceding pages and humble yourself enough to learn from those who've come before you, the possibilities for your impact on this world are near limitless. Your legacy, regardless of where you are in your leadership journey, starts now. The way you start determines how you finish.

The time has come for you to be who God has called you to be, to live out His purpose for your life.

Never let your ambition force you to create a false self. As you lead, share the real you with others.

Root yourself in an untamable love for God. Seek Him first, and let Him handle the lesser things.

As you pursue this calling, make excellence a nonnegotiable. God deserves your best.

When the time comes to take a risk or make a difficult decision, push through the fear. He'll sustain you.

Let your convictions and principles steady you. Hold fast to your integrity, discipline, and humility.

When stress runs high and difficulties arise, keep hoping. Remember that with God on your side, a better tomorrow is possible.

Build bridges, not walls, with those around you. There's power in partnerships.

And finally, don't believe the lie that you are the center of the universe. Seek out older leaders who can help grow you, encourage you, and guide you. And then pour your life into others.

The journey we began together is now yours to complete. Lead now. Lead well. Become the change maker God has called you to be.

YOUNG INFLUENCERS LIST

FIFTY CHANGE MAKERS ON THE RISE

FOR NEARLY FIVE YEARS, I'VE BEEN COMPILING A RUNNING LIST of young change makers who are making a difference. That list now includes over three hundred young leaders. Each of their stories is an example of one or more essentials of the catalyst leader.

Young Influencers List
(over three hundred young leaders you should know)
http://catalystleader.com/younginfluencers

Below I have included fifty of those leaders. This is by no means an exhaustive list of prominent, rising leaders. Instead, it is a sampling of influencers who you may not be familiar with but who are doing amazing work and embody the essentials of a catalyst leader. These are folks I would love for you to know. I've listed them here unranked, in alphabetical order, because of my admiration for them. I encourage you to take time to learn about their organizations and work.

Obviously, with a list like this, organizations change, leaders find new roles, new names emerge, and the list evolves regularly. That is why I update this list on a regular basis every few months. The latest and most updated "Young Influencers List" is available at http://catalystleader.com.

1. Alli Worthington—BlissDom Conference
2. Allison Trowbridge—Not For Sale: End Human Trafficking and Slavery
3. Amanda Ramirez—Johnnyswim
4. Angie Smith—speaker and author
5. Anthony Bradley—author and professor at King's College
6. Beth Murray—*Today Show* producer
7. Bianca Olthoff—the A21 Campaign
8. Brad Jones—Passion Conferences
9. Brian Wurzell—Slingshot Group
10. Caitlin Crosby—the Giving Keys
11. Carl Lentz—Hillsong Church NYC
12. Courtney Dow—NightLight USA
13. Darren Whitehead—Church of the City

14. Dave Morin—Path
15. Del Chittim—Southeastern University
16. Dhati Lewis—the Rebuild Initiative
17. Erik Lokkesmoe—Different Drummer
18. Iris Liang—Videre
19. Je'Kob Washington—musician, artist, and songwriter
20. Jen Alt—Segel Foundation
21. Jen Hatmaker—church planter, author, and speaker
22. Jenny White—Art House Dallas
23. Jo Saxton—author and speaker
24. Jon Tyson—Trinity Grace Church
25. Joy Eggerichs—Love and Respect NOW
26. Kevin Olusola—cellist, beatboxer, and member of Pentatonix
27. Laura Waters Hinson—filmmaker
28. Leonce Crump—Renovation Church
29. Lindsey Nobles—Food for the Hungry
30. Lori Wilhite—Leading and Loving It
31. Melissa Moore Fitzpatrick—Living Proof Ministries
32. Nicole Baker Fulgham—the Expectations Project
33. Nikki Toyama—Urbana
34. Pedro Garcia—Calvary Chapel Kendall
35. Perrin Rogers—the Triumphant Church
36. Raan Parton—Apolis Clothing
37. Rachel Ramsey Cruze—the Lampo Group
38. Ralph Castillo—Christ Tabernacle, Queens, NY

39. Rebekah Lyons—author and Q
40. Rich Wilkerson Jr.—the Vous!
41. Ryan Sisson—Moniker Group
42. Scott McClellan—Echo Conference
43. Shaun King—HopeMob
44. Tad Agoglia—First Response Team of America
45. Tara Jenkins—Fellowship Missionary Baptist Church
46. Tara Teng—Miss Canada 2011
47. Thea Ramirez—Adoption-Share
48. Tommy Kyllonen—Crossover Church
49. Travis Mason—Google
50. Trip Lee—singer, songwriter, and hip-hop artist

APPENDIX

"TODAY'S CHRISTIAN LEADERS" STUDY, IN PARTNERSHIP WITH BARNA RESEARCH GROUP

THE FOLLOWING SURVEY RESULTS REFLECT A NATIONWIDE study of Christian adults, ages eighteen and older. It was conducted by Barna Research Group through online surveys of 1,116 self-described Christian adults in June 2012. The study probes the essentials discussed in this book. The following is a sampling of the results of this study.

1. WHAT KIND OF LEADERS ARE NEEDED?

The first question explored what Christians believe to be the most important traits that leaders need to possess given all the changes taking place in the world. Respondents were given ten different options, including short descriptions, to choose from:

1. Courage—*being willing to take risks*
2. Vision—*knowing where you are going*
3. Competence—*being good at what you do*
4. Humility—*giving credit to others*
5. Collaboration—*working well with others*
6. Passion for God—*loving God more than anything else*
7. Integrity—*doing the right thing*
8. Authenticity—*being truthful and reliable*
9. Purpose—*being made for or "called" to the job*
10. Discipline—*the ability to stay focused and get things done*

Of those ten characteristics listed, most Christians believe that integrity is the most important characteristic for leaders today (64%). On the next tier are authenticity (40%) and discipline (38%), which are followed by passion for God (31%) and competence (31%). The least important factors are purpose (5%) and humility (7%). Vision (26%), collaboration (25%), and courage (15%) are ranked in the middle of the pack.

Evangelicals are a subset of the broader Christian market, comprising 8 percent of the nation's population. They are more likely to identify the importance of passion for God and integrity, but they are less likely than other Christians to name discipline, competence, vision, or collaboration.

Older Christians are more likely than their younger peers (under 40) to list integrity, authenticity, passion for God, and courage as critical facets of leadership. Younger leaders are slightly more likely to name vision, collaboration, and humility. Still, the differences between the age groups are not great.

Table 1: Most Important Leadership Traits

Question: Thinking about all the changes taking place in our nation and the world, what will be the 2 or 3 most important leadership traits for people to be great leaders in the next decade? (Mark between 1 and 3 responses.)

	ALL CHRISTIANS	EVANGELICALS	AGE GROUP		SELF-DESCRIBED LEADER	
			18–39	40-plus	yes	no
integrity	64%	75%	59%	66%	65%	63%
authenticity	40	41	34	42	39	41
discipline	38	22	41	37	36	41
passion for God	31	83	26	34	33	28
competence	31	14	33	30	31	32
vision	26	16	29	25	29	23
collaboration	25	15	27	23	24	25
courage	15	13	10	17	17	13
humility	7	7	9	5	6	7
purpose	5	6	3	6	5	4
n=	*1107*	*87*	*352*	*755*	*635*	*469*

2. THE BOSSES WE WANT TO WORK FOR

In this era of increasing importance of good jobs, Christians were also asked what kind of boss they would like to work for. Respondents were given the same ten items to choose from. Interestingly, the same top two characteristics emerge as when asked to identify the most important leadership traits needed today: integrity (57%) and authenticity (47%).

But after that, the lists are different. Instead of the #3 to #5 factors being discipline, passion for God, and competence, Christians say they would want to work for a boss who is collaborative, competent, and humble. Passion for God drops from fourth place to seventh position, perhaps reflecting people's realization that the workplace is not necessarily filled with believers. Still, among evangelicals, finding a boss who is a believer remains the most important criterion in their job search.

Younger leaders are less likely than their older peers to look for bosses who have integrity or authenticity, but are slightly more interested in collaboration and purpose. They are much more likely than older adults to look for bosses who are humble.

What stood out among people who consider themselves to be leaders is that they are more interested than normal in serving for other leaders who live with integrity and lead with clear vision.

Table 2: Characteristics of a Potential Boss

Question: Suppose you are offered a job from two different companies and you have to choose between two different kinds of bosses.

Remember, not everyone is perfect, but what are the 2 or 3 characteristics of the boss you would be most interested in working for? (Mark between 1 and 3 responses.)

	ALL CHRISTIANS	EVANGELICALS	AGE GROUP		SELF-DESCRIBED LEADER	
			18–39	40-plus	yes	no
integrity	57%	63%	51%	59%	59%	54%
authenticity	47	54	36	52	45	49
collaboration	39	15	41	37	36	42
competence	37	24	38	37	39	35
humility	26	27	32	23	23	30
vision	22	12	22	22	25	17
passion for God	22	68	20	22	22	20
discipline	22	15	25	21	24	20
courage	5	3	3	6	6	4
purpose	5	7	8	4	4	7
n=	*1109*	*87*	*352*	*757*	*636*	*469*

3. SELF-DESCRIBED LEADERS

Overall, more than half of Christians in this country say they are leaders (58%). About the same proportion of evangelicals (55%) believe they are leaders. There is no statistically significant difference based on the age of those interviewed.

The box below shows the demographic, theolographic, and psychographics of today's self-identified leaders.

It is somewhat striking that so few leaders think they have the kinds of leadership traits that are most needed today (i.e., integrity and authenticity). Or, to put it differently, they think of themselves as competent, disciplined collaborators, although those three traits are ranked as fifth, seventh, and third most important, respectively, in what is really needed today.

Table 3: Self-Described Leader

Question: Do you personally consider yourself to be a leader?

	ALL CHRISTIANS	EVANGELICALS	AGE GROUP		SELF-DESCRIBED LEADER	
			18–39	40-plus	yes	no
yes	58%	55%	59%	57%	100%	0%
no	43	45	41	43	0	100
n=	*1111*	*87*	*355*	*756*	*639*	*472*

4. HOW LEADERS EVALUATE THEMSELVES

Among those respondents who identified themselves as leaders, the survey asked them to evaluate the *one* quality that best defines their leadership. The highest-ranked trait is competence (20%), followed by discipline (16%), collaboration (15%), integrity (15%), and authenticity (14%). Appropriately, only 1 percent of Christians say they are best at being humble.

Evangelicals are cut from a different bolt of cloth, naming passion for God as far and away their best leadership quality (42%).

There are not any substantial differences by age group, with the only notable difference being that older leaders are actually slightly more likely than younger leaders to name authenticity (16% versus 11%, respectively).

Table 3a: Personal Leadership Qualities

Question: Which *one* of the following leadership qualities best defines you?

	ALL CHRISTIANS	EVANGELICALS	AGE GROUP		SELF-DESCRIBED LEADER	
			18–39	40-plus	yes	no
competence	20%	4%	19%	20%	20%	NA
discipline	16	8	20	15	16	NA
collaboration	15	11	13	16	15	NA
integrity	15	15	15	14	15	NA
authenticity	14	12	9	16	14	NA
passion for God	11	42	13	11	11	NA
vision	4	2	4	4	4	NA
purpose	3	2	5	2	3	NA
courage	2	*	1	2	2	NA
humility	1	4	2	1	1	NA
n=	*636*	*48*	*208*	*428*	*636*	*NA*

*indicates less than one-half of one percent

Leaders were also asked what they would most like to improve, using the same list of ten traits. The area where they want the most help is courage (27%), which is followed by a desire to grow in terms of discipline (17%), vision (15%), and passion for God (13%).

Evangelical leaders are most similar to the broader Christian market in this respect: they want to grow in terms of courage (27%), discipline (25%), passion for God (14%), and vision (9%). Younger leaders express a greater desire than older leaders to grow in terms of vision and purpose.

Table 3b: Personal Leadership Qualities That Need Improvement

Question: Which *one* of the following qualities needs the most improvement in your own leadership?

	ALL CHRISTIANS	EVANGELICALS	AGE GROUP		SELF-DESCRIBED LEADER	
			18–39	40-plus	yes	no
courage	27%	27%	25%	28%	27%	NA
discipline	17	25	17	17	17	NA
vision	15	9	20	12	15	NA
passion for God	13	14	10	14	13	NA
collaboration	9	4	10	9	9	NA
purpose	9	8	12	8	9	NA
humility	5	8	5	5	5	NA
competence	2	4	1	3	2	NA
integrity	2	2	1	3	2	NA

	ALL CHRISTIANS	EVANGELICALS	AGE GROUP		SELF-DESCRIBED LEADER	
			18–39	40-plus	yes	no
authenticity	1	0	1	1	1	NA
n=	627	48	203	424	627	NA

5. ATTITUDES ABOUT WORK, CALLING, AND LEADERSHIP

Finally, the research probed a number of different attitudes among Christians about work, calling, and leadership, set up as a series of agree/disagree statements.

Overall, 82 percent of Christians in America believe the nation is facing a crisis of leadership because there are not enough good leaders right now. Among evangelicals, 94 percent believe this to be true. Older Christians (84%) are most likely to assert this perspective, but the vast majority of younger Christians (78%) concur.

Most Christians (67%) believe the work they are doing is helping to create a better world; however, only one-fifth strongly agree. Evangelicals are even more sanguine about their efforts (82%) than the norm. The gap between younger (65%) and older Christians (68%) is statistically indistinct; yet, younger Christians are more likely than average to *strongly* concur with the statement (27%), perhaps reflecting the growing sensibility of "doing good" in the world.

When looking at the broad patterns, a sense of pride

in their work was nearly a universal sentiment (98%). Nevertheless, when looking at the "agree strongly" response line, younger adults, evangelicals, and nonleaders could be criticized for showing some lower-than-average pride in their efforts.

The idea that their workplace has a clear vision that is easily understood by employees is an opinion strongly endorsed by only one-quarter of today's working Christians (23%). Evangelicals (35%) are slightly higher than normal, but the basic findings show that most people have only modest confidence or clarity about their company's vision.

Another survey question probed this opinion: the belief that God is calling them to do something else in terms of work, but they have not been willing to make a change yet because of their current life situation. Overall, 9 percent of working Christians agreed strongly and another 26 percent agreed somewhat, totaling one-third of today's employed Christians (35%) who are experiencing this kind of tension. Among younger Christians, nearly half (44%) are feeling this disconnect between the profession or job they would like and the realities of their current situation.

When asked if they believe that a person's calling lasts a lifetime, on balance, most people disagree rather than agree (68% versus 32%). In fact, only 4 percent strongly agree that one can see what a person is called to do from an early age. There are no notable differences by age, evangelical commitment, or leader status. Yet, instead of being an area where people have strongly formed opinions, it appears that most Christians just have not given this matter much thought. (Notice that most of the respondents choose the middle-ground answers of "somewhat," reflecting hedged bets.)

Choosing to interact regularly with an older mentor who gives great advice about work is even less common than having clear vision at work—only 16 percent of working Christians firmly assert they have this type of relational work-related guidance in place. Younger Christians are slightly more likely than older believers to have such mentorship in their lives (22% versus 12%), but there is still considerable room for growth. Interestingly, those who are leaders are twice as likely as nonleaders to say they have an older mentor in place to help navigate professional issues.

Table 5a: Feel Called to Their Work

Question: Thinking about your current work, do you feel that you are "made for" or "called" to the work you currently do?

AMONG THOSE EMPLOYED	ALL CHRISTIANS	EVANGELICALS	AGE GROUP		SELF-DESCRIBED LEADER	
			18–39	40–plus	yes	no
feel "called" to my current work	34%	55%	31%	36%	38%	27%
do not feel called	19	18	27	14	18	21

AMONG THOSE EMPLOYED	ALL CHRISTIANS	EVANGELICALS	AGE GROUP		SELF-DESCRIBED LEADER	
			18–39	40–plus	yes	no
not sure	13	16	16	12	13	15
never thought about it before	34	11	26	38	32	38
n=	593	47	216	377	383	211

Only about one-third of Christians (34%) feel called to the work they currently do (among those who are currently employed). This is much higher among evangelicals (55%), but still reflects a huge gap in terms of the Christian community's sense of divine purpose in their work.

Others say they "do not feel called" (19%), indicate they are "not sure" (13%), or admit they have "never thought about it before."

Younger Christians are less likely to feel called to their work than older Christians (31% versus 36%); however, interestingly, older Christians are even more likely than the younger set to confess they have never really even considered the idea of being called to their current role (26% versus 38%).

Table 5b: Attitudes about Work, Leadership, and Calling

Question: Do you agree or disagree with the following statements:

ASKED AMONG ALL CHRISTIANS	ALL CHRISTIANS	EVANGELICALS	AGE GROUP		SELF-DESCRIBED LEADER	
			18–39	40-plus	yes	no
the nation is facing a crisis of leadership because there are not enough good leaders right now						
agree strongly	41%	73%	27%	48%	43%	37%
agree somewhat	41	21	51	36	38	45
disagree somewhat	15	4	20	12	14	15
disagree strongly	4	2	2	4	4	3
the work I am doing is helping to create a better world						
agree strongly	20	20	26	17	26	12
agree somewhat	47	62	39	51	49	44
disagree somewhat	24	8	30	22	19	32
disagree strongly	9	10	5	11	7	12
*n**=*	*1116*	*87*	*358*	*758*	*639*	*472*

Table 5c: Attitudes about Work, Leadership, and Calling

Question: Do you agree or disagree with the following statements:

AMONG THOSE EMPLOYED	ALL CHRISTIANS	EVANGELICALS	AGE GROUP		SELF-DESCRIBED LEADER	
			18–39	40-plus	yes	no
I take personal pride in the quality of work that I do						
agree strongly	72%	65%	61%	77%	79%	58%
agree somewhat	26	26	34	21	19	39
disagree somewhat	1	0	2	*	1	1
disagree strongly	1	9	2	1	1	2
the place where I work has a clear vision that is easily understood by those working there						
agree strongly	23	35	27	21	22	24
agree somewhat	48	35	50	46	48	47
disagree somewhat	20	23	15	23	22	17
disagree strongly	9	7	9	10	8	12
I regularly interact with an older mentor who gives me great advice about work						
agree strongly	16	14	22	12	19	10
agree somewhat	33	37	38	30	31	35
disagree somewhat	31	22	25	35	31	31
disagree strongly	21	27	16	23	19	24

AMONG THOSE EMPLOYED	ALL CHRISTIANS	EVANGELICALS	AGE GROUP		SELF-DESCRIBED LEADER	
			18–39	40-plus	yes	no
I feel like God is calling me to do something else in terms of work, but I have not been willing to make a change yet because of my current situation in life						
agree strongly	9	8	12	8	9	10
agree somewhat	26	25	32	23	25	27
disagree somewhat	36	30	32	38	39	30
disagree strongly	29	37	25	31	27	33
$n^{**}=$	595	47	216	377	383	211

* indicates less than one-half of one percent

**sample size varies with each question

NOTES

Introduction / Learning to Lead

1. Donna Fenn, "Cool, Determined, and Under 30," *Inc.*, October 1, 2008.
2. Jon Acuff, "Stuff Christians Life," weblog, http://www.jonacuff .com/stuffchristianslike/
3. Jon Acuff, *Quitter: Closing the Gap between Your Day Job and Your Dream Job* (Nashville: Lampo Press, 2011).

1 / Called

1. Katie Davis, "Kisses from Katie," July 15, 2008; http:// kissesfromkatie.blogspot.com/2008/07/for-last-two-days-i-have-once-again.html.
2. Catalyst podcast, episode 168.
3. In our "Today's Christian Leaders" study, 68% disagreed with the statement "a person's calling lasts a lifetime"; 32% disagreed with the statement.
4. J. R. R. Tolkien, *The Fellowship of the Ring* (Boston: Houghton Mifflin, 1965), 70.
5. John Ortberg, "Guard Your Calling, Frodo," *Leadership Journal*, January 10, 2011; http://www.christianitytoday.com/le/2011/ january-online-only/guardcallingfrodo.html.

2 / Authentic

1. Mark Batterson, Catalyst podcast, episode 160, http://www.catalystspace.com/content/podcast/catalyst_podcast_episode_160/.
2. Bob Goff, *Love Does* (Nashville: Thomas Nelson, 2012).
3. Claire Diaz Ortiz, Catalyst Dallas, 2012.
4. Rick Warren, Catalyst podcast, episode 168, http://www.catalystspace.com/content/podcast/catalyst_podcast_episode_168/.

3 / Passionate

1. As told by Tullian Tchivjian, "Our Calling, Our Spheres," *Leadership Journal*, September 6, 2010; http://www.christianitytoday.com/le/2010/summer/ourcallingspheres.html.
2. David Platt, Catalyst podcast, episode 170.
3. Margaret Feinberg, *Wonderstruck: Awaken to the Nearness of God* (Nashville: Worthy Publishing, 2012), 7.
4. Louie Giglio, Catalyst podcast, episode 173, http://www.catalystspace.com/content/podcast/catalyst_podcast_episode_173/.
5. Francis Chan, Catalyst podcast, episode 152, http://www.catalystspace.com/content/podcast/catalyst_podcast_episode_152/.
6. Bill Hybels, Catalyst podcast, episode 161, http://www.catalystspace.com/content/podcast/catalyst_podcast_episode_161/.

4 / Capable

1. Holly Green, "Redefining Excellence for Today's World," Forbes, March 6, 2012; http://www.forbes.com/sites/work-in-progress/2012/03/06/redefining-excellence-for-todays-world/
2. Perry Noble, "Four Problems the Church Has Got to Deal With!" April 19, 2012; http://www.perrynoble.com/2012/04/19/four-problems-the-church-has-got-to-deal-with/.
3. Nancy Ortberg, Catalyst West, 2011.

5 / Courageous

1. Tad Agoglia, Catalyst Atlanta, 2011.
2. Jamie Walters, "Courage: Tap Greater Potential and Thrive Through Challenges," *Inc.*, March 1, 2002; http://www.inc.com/articles/2002/03/23995.html.

3. Rick Warren, Catalyst podcast, episode 168, http://www.catalystspace.com/content/podcast/catalyst_podcast_episode_168/.

4. Andy Stanley, Catalyst podcast, episode 176, http://www.catalystspace.com/content/podcast/catalyst_podcast_episode_176/.

5. Gilbert Keith Chesterton, *Orthodoxy*, (London: John Lane Company, 1909) 170.

6 | Principled

1. Walter Isaacson, *Steve Jobs* (New York: Simon & Schuster), 6.

2. Rick Warren, Catalyst podcast, episode 168, http://www.catalystspace.com/content/podcast/catalyst_podcast_episode_168/.

3. Eugene Cho, Catalyst Dallas, 2011.

4. As told by Tullian Tchivjian, "Our Calling, Our Spheres," *Leadership Journal*, September 6, 2010; http://www.christianitytoday.com/le/2010/summer/ourcallingspheres.html.

5. Christy Nockels, Catalyst podcast, episode 185, http://www.catalystspace.com/content/podcast/catalyst_podcast_episode_185/.

6. Jim Collins, Catalyst Atlanta, 2011.

7. Louie Giglio, Catalyst podcast, episode 173, http://www.catalystspace.com/content/podcast/catalyst_podcast_episode_173/.

8. Don Yaeger, "Lessons from Sports: Nolan Ryan's Longevity," *Success Magazine,* http://www.success.com/articles/1114-lessons-from-sports-nolan-ryan-s-longevity.

9. Ibid.

10. Pete Wilson, Catalyst podcast, episode 189, http://www.catalystspace.com/content/podcast/catalyst_podcast_episode_189/.

11. Christy Nockels, Catalyst podcast, episode 185, http://www.catalystspace.com/content/podcast/catalyst_podcast_episode_185/.

12. Dallas Willard, Renovation of the Heart (Colorado Springs, CO: NavPress, 2002), 254.

13. Malcolm Gladwell, Outliers (New York: Hachette, 2008), 41.

14. Jim Collins and Morten T. Hansen, Great by Choice (New York: HarperBusiness, 2011), 41.

15. Louie Giglio, Catalyst podcast, episode 173, http://www.catalystspace.com/content/podcast/catalyst_podcast_episode_173/.

16. John Maxwell, 21 Irrefutable Laws of Leadership (Nashville, TN: Thomas Nelson, 1998).

17. David Weinberger, "The American Leader's Love Affair with Integrity," *Harvard Business Review*, October 29, 2010.

18. As defined by Paul Klein in "What's Your Return on Integrity," *Forbes*, June 6, 2011; http://www.forbes.com/sites/csr/2011/06/06/whats-your-return-on-integrity/.

19. Andy Stanley, "Integrity at Risk," Catalyst GroupZine (Nelson Impact, 2007).

7 | Hopeful

1. Esther Havens, Catalyst Dallas, 2012.

2. Bill Hybels, Catalyst podcast, episode 161, http://www.catalystspace.com/content/podcast/catalyst_podcast_episode_161/.

3. So much of this spirit of vision and hopefulness for Catalyst we've learned from Reggie Joiner. Reggie truly believes in the next generation, and has inspired hope through his work.

8 | Collaborative

1. Jack Dorsey, Catalyst West, 2011.

2. Larry Prusak, "The One Thing that Makes Collaboration Work," *Harvard Business Review*, http://blogs.hbr.org/cs/2011/07/one_thing_that_makes_collaboration.html.

3. As quoted by Jacob Morgan, "4 Reasons Your Company Needs a Collaboration Upgrade, Stat," *FastCompany*, http://www.fastcompany.com/1842473/4-reasons-your-company-needs-collaboration-upgrade-stat.

4. Chris Anderson, *Free*, (New York: Hyperion, 2009).

5. John M. Caddell, "Randy Nelson of Pixar: Collaboration is Like Improv Theatre," PennLive, August 10, 2010, http://blog.pennlive.com/shoptalkmarketing/2010/08/randy_nelson_of_pixar_collabor.html.

ACKNOWLEDGMENTS

THIS IS NOT A BOOK. YOU'RE HOLDING IN YOUR HANDS A journey. And my journey as a leader starts first and foremost with Jesus, whom I passionately love, follow, and confess as Lord and Savior of my life, and who has made me into who I am today. Above all else, Soli Deo Gloria.

As with any journey, there are people who must be thanked for helping me arrive at my destination. Accordingly, I'd like to offer my deepest gratitude to the following people:

First of all, to my parents, Penny and Jerry. My brother, Brian, and sister-in-law, Jody. Your encouragement and support has been priceless. Adam, Carlee, and Jake: I love you and am so proud of you.

To the Catalyst team for working tirelessly together to

impact leaders. You are the best team in the world. I'm honored to serve alongside you. Chad Johnson (aka Squeaky J), Melissa Kruse (aka Mel), Jason Haynes (aka Hover), Tyler Reagin (aka Reaginomics), Sally Sumrall (aka Side Convo), Ansley Souther, Brian Cole, Robby Smith (aka NBC), Julianne Graves (Julz), Jill Walker, Amberly Sykes, Ansley Williams, Joe Shelton, Jon Hout, Daniel Windsor, Stan Johnson, Ashley Williams (aka Ash), and Kevin Lee (Lee Jeans). And to James Vore for stepping in and providing huge help with marketing, creativity, and overall project management. Thanks to you and the entire team for living out humble, hungry, and hustle!

To Jonathan Merritt, for walking with me and helping to craft this project.

To my assistant, Michelle Hoeft, for reading the manuscript, watching lots of video, giving great feedback, keeping me focused, and being awesome.

To Jeff Shinabarger for pushing me to make this book a reality. You continue to move the needle and create hope. We started these projects together. Thanks for being on the journey.

To Gabe Lyons, Ken Coleman, Jason Locy, and Tim Willard for being such great friends and my inner circle. Your advice, perspective, honesty, and feedback are priceless.

To Jeremie Kubicek and Matthew Myers for the green light to push this forward. And for giving me the resources and opportunity to try our best to change the world!

To Andy Stanley, Louie Giglio, and Craig Groeschel for your friendship and inspiration.

To Chris Ferebee, a great literary agent and a great friend. Thanks for being an advocate and an adviser. Much more to do together.

To John Maxwell for your mentoring and legacy. I'm a better leader because of you.

To Mark Cole, for giving me a chance to lead Catalyst way back when. Thanks for believing in me.

To Reggie Joiner and Lanny Donoho. I stand on the shoulders of giants. Both of you have taught me so much about events, programming, leadership, and authenticity.

To Carlos Whittaker, Tyler Stanton, Tripp Crosby, Brian Pirkle, Jonathan Bostic, Ryan Shove, and our entire programming and creative team. Thanks for helping us create amazing leadership experiences!

To Bob Foster Sr. for the many breakfasts together on the south porch at Lost Valley. Your investments are still paying dividends.

To Steve Graves and Tom Addington, who taught me so much about business and leadership.

To Margaret Feinberg, for expert writing advice, editorial direction, and honest feedback. And to Lysa TerKeurst and Mike Foster for the many conversations and helpful advice and encouragement to push this project forward.

To my aunt Brenda and uncle Mike, who put up with lots of antics from my brother Brian and me over the years.

Ben Martin, Matt Weaver, Patrick O'Neil, Jason Shipman, Billy Blanchard, and Dace Starkweather, for creating a great team at Lost Valley and even better lifelong friendships.

To David Kinnaman and the Barna Research Group team for providing helpful advice, research, and a picture of the future. It's a joy to partner in impacting leaders.

To the entire Thomas Nelson team. To Joel Miller, Brian Hampton, and Michael Hyatt for believing in this project and believing in the next generation of leaders. To Kristen Parrish and Heather Skelton for such great insight into the editorial process. And to Chad Cannon, Katy Boatman, and Brenda Smotherman for marketing ideas, connections, innovation, and strategy.

And to the entire Catalyst community: you inspire me. Your leadership and influence on the front lines is crucial. I'm honored to be on the journey with each of you!

ABOUT THE AUTHOR

BRAD LOMENICK IS LEAD VISIONARY AND PRESIDENT OF Catalyst, one of America's largest movements of young Christian leaders. Catalyst's mission is to equip, inspire, and release the next generation of leaders through events, resources, consulting, content, and connecting. In the last thirteen years, Catalyst has convened hundreds of thousands of leaders through high-energy and experiential conferences across the United States.

Prior to running Catalyst, Brad spent five years involved in the growth of the nationally acclaimed *Life@Work* magazine and was a management consultant with Cornerstone Group, where he worked with a variety of companies, organizations, and nonprofit enterprises. Before that, he served as foreman for Lost Valley Ranch, a four-diamond working guest ranch in the mountains of Colorado.

Brad has had the privilege of interviewing dozens of the world's leading thinkers—including Malcolm Gladwell, Seth Godin, Rick Warren, Jack Dorsey, Dave Ramsey, and more—through the Catalyst podcast, which is free for download on iTunes or at catalystpodcast.com. He blogs about leadership, creativity, innovation, teamwork, personal growth, and more at bradlomenick.com.

Brad serves on the advisory boards for Suffered Enough, the A21 Campaign, Red Eye Inc., and Praxis. He holds a bachelor's degree from the University of Oklahoma and currently resides just outside of Atlanta, Georgia.

You can follow Brad on Twitter at @bradlomenick and connect with Catalyst at catalystconference.com.

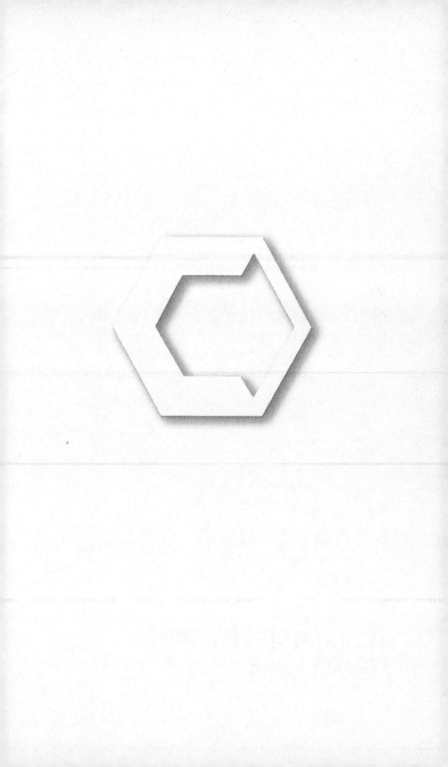

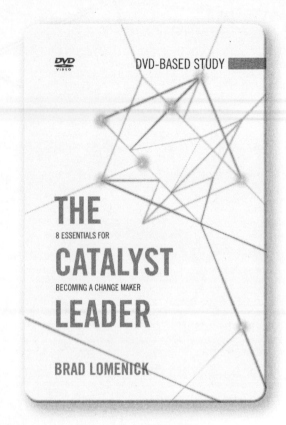

DVD VIDEO

DVD-BASED STUDY

THE
8 ESSENTIALS FOR
CATALYST
BECOMING A CHANGE MAKER
LEADER

BRAD LOMENICK

THE CATALYST LEADER DVD-BASED STUDY KIT

8 ESSENTIALS FOR BECOMING A CHANGE MAKER

The Catalyst Leader DVD-Based Study identifies the 8 essentials and key characteristics for leading well now and over the next 20 years. Are you a high-octane, energizing leader with big ideas and the skills to back them up? Do you help shape the hearts and minds of those you lead? In short, are you a Catalyst leader? The reality is that most of us want to be good leaders, but we're not sure how to use those elements to best impact our leadership.

You may be a leader, but are you influencing and truly making a difference? *The Catalyst Leader* is a brand new resource designed to help you lead now and lead well.

DVD Kit includes:

- 8 sessions of study
- Videos for use in a small group or individual setting
- 1 copy of the Participant's Guide

Additional copies of the DVD and Participant's Guide are sold separately.

CATALYST

A CONVERGENCE OF NEXT GENERATION LEADERS